OLD NATIONAL

And Other Inspirational Truths

Timothy L. Fort, PhD, JD

Table of Contents

DEDICATION

To all of my professional mentors over the course of my career. Each of these people, along with my other mentors, taught me to recognize exemplary conduct while maintain critical analysis.

ACKNOWLEDGMENTS

My deep gratitude to the following members of Team Tim:

Lisa Cornelio, who edited this book and who always makes me sound better than I really am.

Tayler Fisher, one of my favorite former students, who designed the cover.

Kurina Fort, my daughter, who prepared the Index.

ABOUT "YOUR TEAM IS #1"

America was born with skepticism. That's why the framers of the Constitution set up a system of checks and balances. They worried about the potential misdeeds of anyone powerful, so they set up a system in which each branch of government was limited in its actions by the other branches. Perhaps they weren't so Dostoyevskian as to see evil lurking in each person, but they were soberly skeptical. With plenty of misconduct – political, economic, civic, personal – to notice, we have plenty of resources at our disposal to reinforce our skepticism.[1]

Yet, I have always feared that skepticism turns into cynicism. That we aren't just skeptical of others, but we cynically don't believe that any authentic good is possible. While it is important not to be naïve, cynicism also leads to hopelessness. Thus, when I teach business ethics and when I write about how businesses can contribute to peace and stability, I try to offer some hope, some examples, and a theoretical construct of how any person and any organization can (and frequently does) contribute to the good. That philosophy drives this book series and it too is something America was born with: optimism.

"Your Team #1" is about recognizing that there is in all of us a sense of goodness that is worth seeing and celebrating. In doing so, we don't give ourselves permission to do bad things – kind of a psychological compensation mechanism – but remind ourselves that we can, indeed, achieve good things. Sometimes, in this age of cynicism, we might think we can't do these good things, but it's within us – indeed, theologically, I believe that a universal Spirit of goodness has planted within us – a capability to do inspiring things, even in cynical times.

We can find these good things in our sports teams, our local schools, our businesses, our families; heck, we can even find them in our pets. This book series is dedicated to chronicling and celebrating these capabilities and actions.

As I will describe in the first chapter, I have wanted to write about Old National Bank for some time because it is a great example of the good things a company can do. While I may write additional books in this series myself, my hope is that other authors will be interested in contributing to this book series with examples and stories telling us how their team, school, business, etc. are also #1.

INTRODUCTION/PREFACE

How I Found ONB

Old National Bank may well be one of the most important companies in the world. Why would a bank in Evansville, Indiana be thought of in such august terms? Well, because it is a bank that has a history of and a current reputation for being an authentic, ethical company while also being quite a bit more than a Mom and Pop store. ONB is closing in on being a $20 billion company. That may not challenge Apple or ExxonMobil, but $20 billion represents a serious company.

At the same time, it is also a community bank, immersed first in Evansville and now in cities in five states. When you ask its stakeholders – and I did – what they admire about the bank, they will tell you stories of an institution that sounds more like a local general store. One of those stakeholders captured things quite succinctly:

> Old National has a nice niche where they are a larger bank, giving them the resources and talent to be competitive in the market place, but also have the culture, feel, and responsiveness of a small Community Bank. This has worked out well for ONB thus far. It will be interesting to see how the culture and mindset develops and changes as the company continues to grow and needs to diversify into more complex products and business units (mezzanine financing, structured finance, investment banking, etc.), as other large banks such as Huntington, B of A,

etc. have.

The challenge of being a large institution practicing community values intrigues me. I grew up on a farm outside of a very tiny town in next-door Illinois. As a youth and later as a lawyer, I found our county's community banks to be, well, inspiring. The Bank of Stronghurst, the Raritan State Bank, the First State Bank of Biggsville were led by people you would have to call community activists. These banks' leaders lead all sorts of civic efforts. Long before anyone talked about "corporate social responsibility," these leaders were not just fiscally sponsoring the parks, senior citizen centers, and Little League teams; they were physically participating in these efforts.

Moreover, employees were not labor inputs; they were the individuals the bank's CEO sat beside at church. The Vice-President's grandson might well be teammates on the baseball team or a fellow trombone player with the janitor's son. The teller's wife might coach the cashier's daughter on the basketball team or direct the choir whose lead alto was the farm loan manager. Thick relationships like these make for a different culture in the workplace than if the only time the same people interacted was at work.

My first bank accounts, starting at about the age of five, were with these banks. Years later, they were my first corporate clients after I joined my father in the practice of law in the local community. One of my first projects for two of these banks was to help them redesign their retirement plans. I was too naïve to know that I couldn't possibly do the job, which is probably why I ended up being able to do it.

Retirement plan conversions are tricky things and sometimes companies undertake the conversion to the detriment of their own employees. That is, the companies reduce what they have to pay for their employee's retirement and, if there is any excess after changing their plans around, the companies pocket the difference.

Not these banks. All the money went to the employees' new plan. The banks also paid me for as much time as was necessary to explain to any employee who had a question how the new plan would work. They made my job easy by providing far more money to the employees than they were legally required to do. They could have taken the money in the retirement funds to fatten the bottom line. They didn't. They could have told the person to figure out the program themselves. They didn't. They went above and beyond and that's what community banking is all about.

Years later, when I became a professor of business ethics, I was challenged to provide examples of companies that really were ethical. The folks posing these challenges believed that businesses were only about the money and business ethics was, as the old (really old) joke goes, an oxymoron. (It's amazing how clever people think they are when they crack that line or its sibling: *business ethics must be a short subject*.) Well, my answer – my examples – were these community banks. I could be very concrete as to why these banks were ethical exemplars.

When a cynic is met with such a response, they often get even crabbier and find themselves eager to dismiss or demonize the example. In my case, it was the dismissal. "Well, those are small companies in little towns." "That's not the real world." I found that a bit odd because my small town seemed pretty real. If you walked into a building, you were inside some structure; it wasn't a hologram. If you withdrew money from the bank, there were real dollars in your hand. How is that not real? But of course these examples don't fit the neat stereotype that *business is bad*, which is a theme saturating our society.

Don't believe me? Name five films made in the last fifty years that positively portray business.[2] For that matter, name two children's movies that positively portray business. You can get back to me when you have the results. I won't wait by the phone.

As my career as a professor of business ethics grew, first as a tenured professor at the University of Michigan, then at George Washington University and now at Indiana University, I still used these small banks as examples of good, ethical businesses. At the same time, I saw the point of the cynics, especially when it came to the financial services industry.

After the mortgage meltdown in 2007-2008, I was on the *Kojo Nnamdi Show* on National Public Radio in Washington. The topic was whether business school education perpetuated the profits-only driver that explained a lot of the corporate misconduct and, frankly, exploitation that pushed the country into its deepest recession since the Great Depression of the 1930s. A professor of business ethics has his job because there is a lot of corporate misconduct – otherwise, one wouldn't need a business ethicist –so I had plenty of ammunition and championed the mission of my own field as an antidote to the problem the NPR program was addressing.

Yet, there were also those community banks back in the Midwest within me. I knew there were good businesses and good business people out there. And so when the host, Kojo, pumped into the airways a scene from *Back to School,* I winced. In the film, Rodney Dangerfield's character is a successful businessman upbraiding a stuffy professor who is talking about the stuff I talk about. Dangerfield's character chides the professor for not explaining how the real world works: bribes, theft, and who you needed to kiss up to or beat up.

"Isn't that the real world of the way business works, Professor Fort?" the host playfully intoned.

"Well," I responded, "it's the Hollywood depiction of the way businesses work, but I've known a lot of businesspeople and most of the ones I know try to get it right, try to treat their employees and customers well, and try to be honest in their work." Kojo took the comment well and we talked (and sparred) about it for awhile. I had to admit, though, that during my academic career, I didn't have any additional financial services institutions to point to as exemplars that might join my small town banks. There were some others I could talk about: Johnson & Johnson, Whole Foods, Motorola, among others; they all had good stories. But not many banks.

This deficit presented itself even more clearly about a year later. Out of the blue, I received a call from none other than the assistant to Federal Reserve Chairman, Ben Bernanke. Would I work with them to design a program for the Chairman to deliver a set of speeches on the history of the Federal Reserve to students at George Washington University?

We decided to put together a class, "Reflections on the Federal Reserve" with Bernanke leading the first four classes. I then recruited a star-studded faculty from around the GW campus to "reflect" on Bernanke and the Fed. I selected thirty students from a pool of about eighty who applied to be in the course. It became a big event, covered by major media. I've never held a class with TV cameras and klieg lights. I've never had to walk past bomb-sniffing dogs to get to class before either.

Bernanke, I have to admit, could not have been more decent or cooperative. Meeting with him prior to the event, I asked him what his policy was for students using their laptops in class. "It's your class, Professor Fort. I'll follow whatever policy you set." Frankly, I figured someone of his stature and power would not be so deferential, but as a former professor himself, he completely respected the integrity of the classroom.

He also told me that each lecture was fifty minutes long. This caused me some concern, because we had seventy-minutes for each class. His leaving to attend to world affairs didn't concern me. What worried me was whether the reporters and cameramen would make a ruckus taking down their equipment as soon as Bernanke left the room.

Then it struck me. "Mr. Chairman," I said. "If you need to leave after fifty minutes, that's fine. But I don't think you will. You are an old professor and once you get into the classroom, you are going to stay there until the final minute because you're going to have a good time."

He shrugged and smiled, but said nothing. He proved me right. He was there until the end.

Actually, Bernanke reminded me a great deal of the leaders of those small town banks. When waiting for my first appointment him, I nervously paced at the security entrance. A guard asked me if I was going to meet the Chairman. After I said yes, the guard said, "you have no reason to be nervous. He is the nicest, most decent man you have ever met. He comes down to the cafeteria and eats with us sometimes; you'd never know he is some important guy. He acts like he is just one of us." Just like those small town bankers.

Maybe that was because Bernanke was a small town fellow from South Carolina. Yet he had travelled to the heights of global power and managed to maintain his demeanor and personal character traits. This itself was something to ponder. How does one do that?

The juxtaposition of his traits was in stark contrast to an op-ed written by a leading executive of Goldman Sachs and published in *The New York Times* just a week before my class began. Greg Smith portrayed a culture in which individuals made money by, according to him, ripping off their own clients. The idea was not to service their clients, but to shake them down. Summarizing his message, Smith wrote: "It astounds me how little senior management gets a basic truth: If clients don't trust you they will eventually stop doing business with you. It doesn't matter how smart you are."[3]

This scenario is about as far away from a community bank as I could imagine, but in the aftermath of the mortgage meltdown, it seemed to capture the real world – there's that term again – of what business (and especially financial services firms) are really all about. They aren't about the dignity of employees. They certainly aren't about community engagement. Heck, they aren't even about looking out for the well-being of their own clients.

With that backdrop, the class began with Bernanke laying out a very complete history of the Federal Reserve, its past incarnations and mistakes and also a rationale for why he, Bernanke, acted as he did during the mortgage meltdown to keep the financial system liquid. It's complex stuff, but whether or not one agreed with Bernanke, he taught his history lesson well. At the end of his last lecture, though, a student asked him a question. She told him she thought he had done a great job explaining the complexities of the Fed and the banking system, but she wondered how this history made a difference on Main Street.[4]

My student's questions brought me full circle, from the heights of co-teaching with the Chairman of the Federal Reserve and the intricacies of international finance (which I still only dimly understand) to what I did understand: Main Street Banking. But here too was a man who impressed me, not as an economist or Fed leader (although there were those aspects too), but as someone who seemed as authentic as they come.

During the build up to the class, I figured I should study up on some financial things to see if I could find some exemplary institutions. I didn't have much luck, but I did find a ranking from Ethisphere Magazine, for whom I sometimes write, naming a bank in Indiana as a "World's Most Ethical Company:" Old National Bank. Huh, I thought. Kind of interesting, but sounds like another one of my little hometown banks.

A year later, I found myself in negotiations with Indiana University to make the move from Washington to the Kelley School of Business. I continued to do some work for Ethisphere, nominated people for their list of influential individuals in the field of ethics, and I continued to notice Old National's recognition as a World's Most Ethical Company.

I also noticed that Old National wasn't exactly like my little hometown banks. At best, my hometown banks' assets might make it up to $100 million. Old National's assets are closing in on $20 billion. $20 billion is a lot of money. They may call themselves a community bank, but this is a good-sized financial institution. And it struck me that Old National Bank was a great proving ground for whether a bank – or any company – could maintain its ethical character while being a big, publicly held company.

And that's why Old National Bank may be one of the most important companies in the world. It's part small-town and community-oriented, and it is part market player on a much bigger stage. One can acknowledge my hometown banks being ethical. One can cringe at the culture that caused Greg Smith's resignation from Goldman Sachs. What's in between? And might that in-between teach us some lessons of how to blend these two seemingly antipodal worlds?

After I had gotten myself settled in Indiana, I decided to make the trip to Evansville to meet CEO Bob Jones and interview him for another book I was writing. Bob introduced me to others at ONB, including Mark Bradford, the regional CEO for ONB's Indianapolis and North Central Indiana branches. Mark appointed me to those branches' advisory board, which gave me more of a front row seat.

The appointment to an ONB board, I have to acknowledge, provides a slight conflict of interest. No, the $600 per quarterly meeting doesn't especially trigger concern, but as an Advisory Board member, I do have a reason to want to see ONB succeed even though I, at least at this writing, own no stock in the company. If this is a book about ONB's ethical dimensions, I have to acknowledge this conflict although I think it is slight enough to not interfere with an independent assessment of how ONB works.

In writing this book, I have drawn on four sources. The first source is my own work. I use three models for analyzing ethical development and conduct in individuals and organizations. The basic model is what I call Total Integrity Management (TIM, for short, although my wife winces at that acronym, calling it disturbingly narcissistic.) This is comprised of three kinds of ways in which people trust an individual or company.

Hard Trust is about complying with the law and/or public opinion. Stakeholders trust a company when it follows the law and companies also generate their own laws – company policies – that can instill trust if the rules are clearly articulated and applied even handedly.

Most of the time when people talk about building trust in business, they are talking about Real Trust. **Real Trust** is about building reputation and social capital. If you treat your employees and customers well, they will want to continue to work with you. This category is about how ethics pays off, which empirical studies generally show is true.

The final category is **Good Trust**. People really trust others when they know that a person is doing ethical things simply because that person really believes those things are important. A person might be honest, for example, simply because they believe that being honest is important regardless whether it helps their reputation or not.

Actually, if there is not some level of Good Trust, the

other trusts don't amount to much. If a person or company doesn't care about ethics in the first place, then they won't be motivated to obey the law or to be concerned with reputation. But beyond being a catalyst for Hard and Real Trust, Good Trust stands as its own reason to trust another person. You trust them (or it, in the case of a company) because you can tell that they believe ethics is an independently important thing for that person to practice.

At the heart of Good Trust, which is mostly what I write about in the ethics field, is a sense of sincerity. In fact, it was because I was co-authoring a book for Stanford University Press entitled *The Sincerity Edge* that I interviewed ONB's Bob Jones. Bob confirmed a long-standing belief of mine: that ethics has its biggest payoff (Real Trust) when ethics are pursued sincerely as independently valuable things (Good Trust). Being ethical to make more money has some merit, but a person or company becomes even more trusted when stakeholders know that ethics are sincerely pursued for their own right.

In that book, *The Sincerity Edge*, my co-author and I interviewed twenty CEOs and/or board members in North America and Europe. They told us what they thought the most important practices are, the most important factors in integrating ethics into a company, and the most important virtues in running and ethical business. We folded those into the categories of Hard, Real and Good Trust; I'll talk about how those characterize ONB's culture as well.[5]

The second source for my work comes from the results of a survey I conducted with ONB employees. The company allowed me to send an invitation to participate in a survey, which employees could complete anonymously. They could also identify themselves if they chose. This wasn't like a typical survey with multiple choice questions. I asked respondents to write out answers telling me a story of something that had inspired them at ONB, why they thought ONB was successful (however they defined success) and an odd question: the color with which they associate ONB. With sixty responses, I collected a good number of stories and vignettes that will comprise the heart of this book.

The third source for the book came from interviews with the leadership of ONB: the executives and board members. I conducted these after the surveys because I wanted the surveys to provide a more bottom-up sense of what went on at ONB rather than hearing what the strategies were from the executives. After the executives heard what the respondents said, I wanted their reactions. So I shared with the leadership a draft of this book's manuscript and then rewrote it, integrating their thoughts while not deleting any of the survey's insights, to provide a comprehensive assessment of ONB.

Finally, I received materials from ONB and independent research the history of ONB. ONB has been around awhile and it's worth knowing that history. It is also important in order to understand its corporate culture.

There has long been a philosophical and legal question whether companies are "persons" since they have no soul, they don't "feel" and only take action through the decisions and conduct of flesh and blood human beings. Corporations are artificial constructs and so when we say that ONB is ethical, what the heck can we possibly mean? Culture and history, however, do provide a sense of corporate identity. As companies act through time, they acquire cultural habits that influence the individuals who work for them. Knowing a company's history, then, helps us to understand its culture and identity and that helps us understand its ethical orientation.

Chapter One briefly sets out that history, chronicling a two hundred-year story of the founding of Old National Bank and its progress through the years. In particular, its resilience in times of national economic crisis and its community engagement stand out.

Chapter Two relates the stories told by the stakeholders of Old National. Sincerity and Good Trust resonate here. Some of these stories are very basic and routine. That is not to diminish them. Aristotle said that most of our virtues are so much a part of who we are that they become habits and we are hardly aware of them. That doesn't mean there isn't a great deal of ethical content in those virtues so a routine thing can also be profound. So can more dramatic stories related by the respondents. This is what I call Good Trust.

Chapter Three crosses the bridge between good actions and a growing recognition that these actions might have some kind of payoff. The relationship between the two is not explicit; most of the stories told by the respondents remain focused on the pure goodness of the action, but there is a sense that other stakeholders might want to do business with Old National because of these actions.

Chapter Four relates the stories that clearly show that Old National's actions have a real benefit. They are the essence with which Old National competes in the marketplace. These stories demonstrate the actions that build Old National's reputation in the community. This is what I call Real Trust.

Chapter Five also crosses a bridge. In this case, the stories show not just building of reputation, but how Old National's actions also protect it from negative public reaction. Primarily, that revolves around avoiding bad public opinion.

Chapter Six confronts the law. It was interesting that the stories told by the respondents did not deal with legal concerns. I don't consider that to be a bad thing. When telling stories about what is inspiring and what counts as success, one doesn't necessarily think of complying with the law or staying out of trouble, although that itself is a feat for some companies and individuals. So, my research had to expand here to interviews with ONB leaders and court cases. Of all the chapters, this is the one that surprised me the most because ONB leaders have a very different perspective of the law than what I am accustomed to hearing.

Chapter Seven looks at the Tone at the Top of Old National Bank. *Every single person* I interviewed pointed to the leaders and the CEO as the starting point for ONB's culture. That's not too surprising. In those interviews I conducted for *The Sincerity Edge*, those CEOs also took on the burden of setting the tone and many other studies have argued that tone at the top is critical. Yet, it is not cookie-cutter. Each company is a little different and so to understand ONB's culture, you need to understand ONB's CEO: Bob Jones.

Chapter Two

A History of Resiliency

Following his team's shellacking by the University of Nebraska 40-6, Notre Dame coach Ara Parseghian walked into his stunned team's locker room and said one thing: "Adversity has the effect of eliciting talents which in prosperous circumstances would have lain dormant."[6] Indeed, while we may celebrate our team's successes, what thrills us is when a person, team, business, or community faces adversity and finds a way to pull through.

That kind of resiliency has been a hallmark of Old National Bank's history. While it has been exceptionally prosperous over the years, one of the real markers of its success has been its repeated ability to continue to transact business even during global and national financial crises and while other banks around the country, including the Midwest, were forced to close.

For example, just a few years before the U.S. Civil War, the country was gripped with the "Panic of 1857." Several factors played a role in the Panic, including uncertainty about the amount of gold that backed paper currency. Once the British government's failure to support the amount of paper money in circulation with precious metal reserves was revealed, financial panic hit London and that spread to the U.S. Other factors were in play as well. A ship carrying gold to New York banks sank, further depleting the backing of paper money. In 1857, people realized that the famous "49ers" gold rush into California had ebbed; indeed, the finding of new gold from California had plateaued, placing further pressure on national finances.

Effects cascaded. The Ohio Life Insurance and Trust

Company, a large financial services company, failed, further roiling economic waters, in particular by causing runs on banks in New York and Cincinnati. A speculative bubble involving the expansion of railroads in the west placed further pressure on the market.

Finally, the Supreme Court's decision in the *Dred Scott* case[7] created uncertainty around how and when the western U.S. would be settled and developed, which also impacted prospects for building railroads. The *Scott* decision nullified the Missouri Compromise, which primarily dealt with slavery, but with the federal government's ability to pass laws governing western territories left doubtful, a good deal of economic unease crept into the markets as well.

Though these economic downturns were in far-flown geographic locales, the Midwest was directly affected by the nationwide, roiled markets. In light of the uncertainty in markets and transportation, grain prices fell, dropping from $2.19 in 1855 to only 80 cents in 1858, placing farmers and merchants in severe straights in the Midwest, including Southern Indiana.[8]

Yet, in the face of this downturn, Old National Bank's doors remained opened for business, just as they did during the Mortgage Meltdown of 2007-2008, the Great Depression in the 1930s, and the Panics of 1837, 1873 and 1893. As with the Panic of 1857, the causes for each of these were mixed, but the pressures on a bank such as Old National were the same.

Markets are prone to ebbs and flows as business cycles run their course and as speculation creates bubbles that pop. It is not a problem unique to the U.S. For example, over-exuberance in the Prussian Empire after its 1871 victory over France eventually caught up with Austrian banks in 1873, when they could no longer sustain expectations.[9] The completion of the Suez Canal in 1869 initially hurt British shipping because of the mismatch of Mediterranean winds and British sailing ships; British ports in South Africa fell out of favor as well because of the convenience of Suez and so the British economy suffered.[10]

These international financial issues were all in play during the early 1870s and spilled over to the U.S. Nation-states limited free trade in favor of protectionism as the U.S. dealt with the aftermath of the Civil War and its economic strains. Fires in Chicago in 1871 and Boston the following year further exacerbated domestic economic issues. No bank could have predicted the effects all these far-flung negative events would have on the economy. Surviving them became less an issue of nimbly anticipating short-term developments than it was maintaining a sturdy foundation that could withstand economic turmoil. That Old National's Bank remained open for business during all these crises indicates that, even early in its history, the bank had already built that foundation.[11]

In 1893, another combination of world events pressed on U.S. markets. The failure of major U.S. railroads, the issue of using silver to back currency, European financial issues, and Argentine wheat harvests flung the country into a depression.[12] This crisis capped off a 19th century roller coaster of financial events that ended with, again, Old National Bank remaining open for business.

As with the first major crisis, the Panic of 1837, other financial calamities were all driven by a combination of global events, U.S. political battles, and the status of precious metals behind paper currencies. For example, in 1837, President Andrew Jackson and Nicholas Biddle, who headed the Second Bank of the United States, dueled for control of the country's finances and re-chartering of the Bank, with uncertainty resulting.[13]

One hundred years later, a different financial crisis was driven more by local events than global ones. The Ohio River massively flooded, leaving one million people homeless. In Evansville, the river rose to an astounding 53.74 feet, almost twenty feet above flood level. Both the City of Evansville and the State of Indiana declared martial law to deal with the flooding and recovery; the efforts paid off; Indiana was the only state impacted by the flood that did not suffer a fatality.[14]

If 53.74 feet of water doesn't close things down, then a winter, however bitter and paralyzing, probably isn't going to either. And so during the Winter of 1917-1918, when 68 inches of snow fell in Evansville and the Ohio River remained frozen for seven weeks, ONB only slowed for a bit.[15] Nearly a hundred years later, the Winter of 2013-2014 sent most of the country, including Southern Indiana, for a cold loop as well, but again only until the snow plows dug out the town.[16] And if ice doesn't stop a company, neither will a fire apparently, as ONB and Evansville faced the fire of 1842 and still, well you know the answer now: stayed open for business.

When the Branch Bank at Evansville, which became Old National, was authorized in 1834, the founders may not have had all these panics, floods, and blizzards in mind. Evansville had been founded just 22 years earlier and Indiana became a state in 1816. Yet, they prepared well because it was just three years after the bank's founding that the Panic of 1837 hit the country; the Bank's first charter - the Evansville Branch Bank - was awarded just two years before the Panic of 1857.

It is true that only individuals have virtues. Companies can't possess them. As has long been said, companies have no souls. Yet companies do have identities. A company's identity flows from the people who work for it. With a history of almost 183 years, a company will have employed many people, so that identity will evolve. At the same time, the history of a company helps to form the identity of those working for it later, shaping the ways the company operates far into the future. When you glimpse into ONB's history, you immediately see this virtue of resiliency as something that makes the company stand apart. Resiliency is an essential feature of ONB's identity.

ONB also strives for the virtue of integrity. That's a virtue that needs a little unpacking. Integrity gets tossed around

24

by a lot of folks today. Companies regularly assert that they are committed to integrity, although they rarely define it. In my experience, when pressed, managers, executives and students tend to equate integrity with honesty. That's a good start, but it doesn't fully define integrity.

Aristotle said that a person (or here, a company) is someone who practices a great number of different virtues. It is a holistic concept, which makes sense when you think about the word itself. What is an *integer*? (Sorry, I had to bring you back to your elementary school math!) An *integer* is a whole number. It's not a fraction or a decimal; it's a full, whole number. What does it mean to *integrate*? It means to bring things together, another holistic concept.

A person (or company) with integrity doesn't simply do one thing; it does many things. A person or company with integrity might be resilient; it also might be compassionate, thoughtful, efficient, cooperative, humble, and potentially much else. So if one is aiming for integrity, that's quite an undertaking. If done seriously, aiming for integrity is something to be praised and speaks well for the person or company pursuing it. We are likely to trust a company that isn't just honest, but that makes good quality products and services and is empathetic, community-oriented, and law-abiding.

The dilemma is two-fold. First, being a person or company of integrity is hard. I am sometimes amazed when people ask me to tell them the three or four things they need to do in order to be ethical. Ah, if things would be so simple! Ethics is hard work. It requires thoughtfulness and practice and, yes, resiliency. It might be easier to be a jerk. Then you don't have standards to worry about, you can just be a jerk.

Not many people really want to aim for that though. In fact, as a doctoral student of mine once quipped, he had never seen a corporate website that blared "We aim to be crooks!" Most of us would like to be good people or companies, but only companies and people that are resilient have the intestinal fortitude to make the effort. ONB's ability to face one crisis after the other created a resilient foundation and culture that became a platform for even higher quests.

The other thing that is a bit of a dilemma is that the different virtues and practices that make up integrity sometimes conflict with each other. Take loyalty and honesty. If a friend were to embezzle money, would you be loyal to your friend and not tell anyone or would you be honest and let the right people know? Sometimes, one has to choose between virtues. The virtues themselves may still be good things, but one may be more important at a given time and place.

Aristotle had a term for this. He called it *phronesis*, which is a sense of judgment or wisdom. A wise person knows which virtue is most important at a given time and place. How does someone become wise? Through training, thoughtfulness and practice, all of which is hard work. But as Ara Parseghian said, it is from that hard work that we elicit talents that would have otherwise lain dormant. Later in the book, we'll see just how much hard work ONB puts into trying to get things right.

Old National Bank's history demonstrates some other key values, such as being a good bank, an efficient institution, a thoughtful investor and a careful evaluator of risks. In other words, there are some basic economic practices that any good financial institution ought to be practicing, and *has* to be practicing in order to be successful.

St. Augustine once said that he would prefer to buy shoes from someone who shared his faith. But he still had to have good shoes, so his first criteria is whether or not the shoes were well-made. That's true in business as well. No one will champion and cheer the ethical practices of business more than I will, an ethics professor for over thirty years. Yet the business has to make good shoes. Old National Bank makes good shoes.

Sometimes we take banks and the services they provide for granted but without them, it's difficult for a community or nation to have any degree of economic and political stability. Years ago, I had lunch with a fellow who was high up in the U.S. effort to rebuild the economy of war-ravaged Iraq. His group tried to entice foreign investors to come to Bagdad and invest. He colorfully characterized the questions business people asked when they arrived:

1. Does my cell phone work?
2. Does my ATM work?
3. Is there a decent hotel?[17]

The first question addressed communication with the outside world. If so, s/he could move things. The third question addressed whether or not there was a perch from which to coordinate activities.

The second question was asked if there was a financial system that allowed for the movement of capital. Banks are the foundation of a financial system. Without banks, society cannot trust that a piece of paper with some words and numbers written on it – i.e. a check –means anything. Without banks, such a document would literally not be worth the paper it was written on.

Banks are the intermediary institutions that facilitate commerce so that if I write a check, the person receiving it has reason to believe that the check is worth something. With such confidence and commerce come jobs, homes, and a myriad of other goods and services. Many businesses are important to an economy whether local, regional, or national. But none are more important than a bank. It safeguards money and rather literally, creates money so that constituents can achieve their financial goals and security. At the heart of doing so is trust in the bank's credibility. It's the loss of that trust, through the mortgage meltdown for instance, that is so damaging to individual victims and to society as a whole. On the other hand, a trustworthy bank provides the foundation for security and for growth.

ATMs, cell phones and hotels were probably not on the minds of folks in Evansville in the early part of the 19th Century. But the folks in Iraq were asking the same questions as the residents of 19th Century Evansville. It is difficult to build a business if you can't talk to customers, suppliers, employees and investors. It's tough to build a business if you have no place to hang your hat. And it's tough to build a business unless you can move money.

Prior to Old National Bank's founding, commerce was unstable and erratic in Southern Indiana. Of course, there were farms and ferries, but not factories and other forms of commerce. There were banks, though these institutions were not exactly the kind of financial centers we think of today. Instead, these banks took advantage of sparsely settled lands; it was rare to find dependable banks. Those that existed traded speculative promissory notes and obligations with a gamble of their reliability that seemed right out of the Wild Wild West. In 1834, Indiana was a bit of the Wild Wild West. Remember, 1834 is just fifteen years before the California Gold Rush and thirty years removed from the transcontinental railroad.

In Southern Indiana, however, the business climate settled with the founding of Old National Bank. "Almost immediately after establishing the bank in 1834, Evansville entered into a period of prosperity."[18]   Good banks provide certainty and stability. People can keep their savings safe while also earning interest. A solid bank –one that is well-managed, attracts deposits of citizens and assesses risks of lending clearly – provides a bulwark and catalyst for economic development.

The growth of Evansville, of course, is not due solely to Old National Bank. Many other fine businesses and financial

28

institutions, such as the Orr Iron Company, the Evansville and Crawfordsville Railroad, Mead Johnson, Evansville College (which became the University of Evansville), Ingleheart Mills, the Evansville Shipyard, Hotel McCurdy and many others have played important roles as well. Yet, ONB's record is one that, as already described, not only coincided with a time of prosperity, but also provided a bedrock of stability through the financial crises of the country and the region.[19]

Old National took a further step in leadership when it became a member of the Federal Reserve. The Fed, as Chairman Bernanke instructed my class in 2012, was formed in reaction to the panics that buffeted the country in the 19th Century. The Fed acted as a banker to the banks themselves and as a banker of the last resort. In other words, if a local bank were to fail, the Fed (along with other insurers, such as the FDIC) could step in to make sure that depositors did not lose their money. As a result, the Fed further strengthened local banks such as ONB and allowed banks to loan more for local and regional projects.

Customers, at least in my taxonomy, are one of three crucial stakeholders for a company. The others are the shareholders and the employees. If a company treats these three stakeholder groups right, they generally will do well in getting other stakeholders – such as the community at large, the government, and the environment – right too. Serving these stakeholder groups well has been central to ONB's success, from its founding until today.

The number of employees at Old National has grown from a handful to approximately 3,000,[20] which has its own economic impact. But take this two steps further. First, because of the lending a bank like Old National does in a community, many other businesses exist and by extension, so do many more employees. A bank is an accelerator for businesses and employment.

Second, when a bank like Old National evaluates a

business for a loan, it will assess how well it is run; it might even have some suggestions for how to improve business or people the business owner might consult in order to run the business better. That expert might be an accountant, a lawyer, a strategic marketer or another expert. Such training of management expertise further creates employment opportunities, not just for those expert accountants and lawyers, but for the businesses to grow themselves so they employ more people. This kind of multiplying effect goes well beyond the bank; it has a positive rippling effect throughout the community.

This is not the end of the story. The history of Old National Bank is not just one of a bank undertaking risk assessment to make more profit. Old National's history is that of being a *community* bank; you don't need a Community Reinvestment Act to mandate extra efforts to make local loans when your very identity already requires it.[21] Sometimes that means taking some extra risks.

I remember when I got out of law school and went back to my hometown to practice. For years, citizens had complained that our community had no retirement center or nursing home. According to state assessment needs, we did not need a nursing home, so residents might have to move an hour or more away when they grew older, which made it much harder to visit elderly relatives. I and another fellow –the assistant cashier of one of the local community banks – formed a non-profit that aimed to build a retirement center that provided nursing care. I was 26; Keith was 25. Neither of us had a clue what we were getting ourselves into, which is probably the main reason we accomplished our goal.

Some community-minded residents donated the money that became the working capital for the nursing home. Those community banks I mentioned in the first chapter pitched in to provide us lines of credit. We took part of the donated funds and invested them in U.S. government bonds to offer as security for the banks to lend us the money for the building of the facility. I concocted an argument that allowing the bonds to run to maturity would cover the bank's stated exposure. But of course, that argument underplayed the banks' overall risk.

It didn't matter. The banks appreciated that we worked to raise the money and provide them with the bonds as collateral, and they lent us the money, even though the bonds didn't fully cover the collateral. Why? Well, they were community banks, saw the good the retirement center would provide to the entire county, and had faith we were going to figure out how to make it successful, so they took the risk.

Community banks define what people these days call "corporate citizenship." Usually, people think of this as corporate social responsibility (CSR); that a company goes beyond its interest in profits to do good things, especially if it is good for its public relations. But the idea of a citizen extends CSR more profoundly. It's not that a company thinks of contributing to the community in which it works after it makes its money, though there is something good to be said for that. Nor is it that some companies practice "strategic CSR" in which companies see that being perceived as a good neighbor enhances their long-term profitability, though again, there is something good to be said for that as well.

If you are a citizen, however, you are a *member* of the community in which you operate. Contributing to your community is not beyond what your responsibility is nor is it simply an enlightened money-making strategy. Being a citizen is about *identifying* with your community because you are a member of it. That is the sense in which Old National has operated. Indeed, that is *the* challenge facing ONB today. It has been a member of the Evansville and Southern Indiana community, as I'll explain shortly. Its challenge in the future will be to find a way to be a member of each community in which it operates as it grows larger and spreads across multiple states.

Richard Schlottman, President of the Bank from 1980-1991, said:

> A company benefits when its leaders are involved with
>
> other business leaders in the community. This, also,
>
> is part of our business – to help our community prosper.
>
> We live and work here, so we want it to be the best
>
> possible community.[22]

Perhaps the first concrete example of Old National's citizenship came shortly after its founding in 1834. Two years later, construction for the Wabash-Erie Canal began. Like the Illinois-Michigan Canal that was successfully constructed a few years later, the Wabash-Erie Canal aimed to connect the waterways of Midwest to the Gulf of Mexico. The Illinois-Michigan Canal did so by connecting Lake Michigan to the Illinois River, which drained into the Mississippi and then to the Gulf of Mexico.[23]

Similarly, the Wabash-Erie Canal was designed to connect the waterways of Southern Indiana, which included the Wabash and eventually Ohio rivers which emptied into the Mississippi and Gulf to Lake Erie. The bank loaned the ill-fated project[24] $30,000, a large amount in 1836, especially for a bank that was only two years old. Whether it is best considered now as a donation or a failed loan is less important than the fact that sometimes, when you are a member of a community, you take risks for the benefit of that community. [25]

The bank was in the vanguard again in 1853 when it

loaned $20,000 for the purchase of equipment to build the Evansville and Crawfordsville Railroad. It also took big risks in the 1930s by lending nearly $60 million to oil producers after oil was found in the area.[26] ONB also donated to the country's Civil War effort, area museums and countless other charitable organizations.[27] Indeed, as the voices of employees will demonstrate in later chapters, the philanthropic spirit is powerful at Old National. That spirit includes donations of money, but it also includes donations of sweat and talent, which make it clear that Old National doesn't just give after making a profit, but involves its very physical and human nature in the communities in which it works. That's the mark of a citizen.

Another hallmark of citizenship is obeying the law. Of course, there will always be disputes, but Old National's record does not include many lawsuits or regulatory issues. Two reasons help to explain why ONB has a good record obeying the law.

The first reason is that it takes the law seriously. When I practiced law, I noticed that I had two kinds of clients. One of them wanted to know what the relevant laws were so they could comply with them. The other wanted to know how to get around the laws that existed. Not surprisingly, I enjoyed the first set of clients more than the second. ONB is like those first set of clients.

Second, ONB looks at the law as a floor. The law is the starting point for the bank to know what to do rather than setting out a minimum set of requirements with which to comply. It aims to do better than merely complying with the law.

Indeed, the attitude Old National takes toward the law itself reveals a great deal of its corporate character and identity. In the aftermath of the terrorist attacks of September 11, 2001, Congress beefed up the Bank Secrecy Act.[28] Originally passed in 1970, the Secrecy Act was amended when lawmakers realized that tracking terrorists' money could be an effective way to prevent attacks from happening in the first place and also aid in identifying and finding perpetrators post-attack Though ONB had previously had a solid record of complying with the provisions of the Act, it suddenly faced a problem in 2012 after the Comptroller of the Currency tightened standards.[29] Suddenly ONB's previously exemplary compliance was challenged as falling short.[30]

ONB had to spend approximately $4 million in order to update its infrastructure to comply with the enhanced regulatory requirements. It may be that ONB would be one of the less likely financial institutions a terrorist organization might use to funnel money, but ONB's CEO said, "Despite all of the pain and cost, in the long-run it was good for us."[31]

This too is an example of a citizen. Whenever you're a member of a community, whether it's a family, neighborhood, church or country, things won't always go right, even when you think you have done everything you could. Yet often the community we're in asks more of us. There are lots of ways to face that; you can complain or challenge or even disobey. There are times and places when that is the right thing to do. Sometimes a society's rules or laws need to be challenged and even disobeyed.

Yet, there are other times – usually more frequent – when one says, *OK if this is what is asked of us, we will do it and get better*. That's a refreshing attitude and an approach you don't always expect to hear from the CEO of a publicly-traded company.

It's worth mentioning there is another thing a community-oriented organization does: it produces leaders. ONB has a track record of promoting from the rank and file while also recognizing when it needs to bring in outside expertise. It also means that the ONB experience is one that produces leaders who range beyond ONB and even Evansville itself.

Included in that are bank presidents such as Hugh McCoullough, who was the President of the State Bank of Indiana, of which ONB began as a branch. In 1863, McCullough answered Abraham Lincoln's call for him to become the first U.S. Comptroller of the Currency.[32] Two Orrs also served as bank presidents: Samuel from 1855-1857 and Samuel L. Orr from 1931-1940. Years later, Robert Orr served as Governor of the State of Indiana.[33]

***

It is worth noting that ONB's work is profound at another level. Yes, Old National is a successful financial institution that obeys the law and makes the stakeholders in its community better; being named a World's Most Ethical Company is no fluke. One of the reasons for the consistency of its success lies in the fact that it is also replicating some deep naturalistic impulses. In other words, ONB is not superficial. Its actions and record demonstrate that it "gets it" at a very deep level.

One of the most influential mentors of my career has been a professor at the Katz School of Business at the University of Pittsburgh. William Frederick, a business ethicist, goes way back in grounding his theories of ethics. He talks about issues of thermodynamics and primatology and other scientific findings that are part of our very human and social nature. To simplify for now, Bill argues that in all nature, there are three recurring forces.[34]

The Economizing nature is about the conversion of raw materials into usable forms. For animals, this is digestion; for plants, photosynthesis. To survive, we need to be able to take raw materials and make them useful and nourishing. Business, he argues, serves as something like the metabolism of society. Business takes resources and converts them into things that we need and want. At the heart of any business, as those folks surveying Baghdad knew, is a financial institution that can move

35

money – and make sure an ATM card works.[35]

The Power-aggrandizing dimension is about quests for power. Who gets the corner office? Who is the boss? Who is dominant? Bill is not very optimistic about this dimension, thinking that often such quests have nothing to do either with converting resources in to usable products nor with building community. While I do agree with Bill that there is competition in nature to see which lion becomes head of his pride and that often, quests for power can be very negative, I also think that a sense of order, and following the law, can be beneficial as well.[36]

The Ecologizing function is about the interdependencies we find in communities that weave us together. A rain forest is replete with these mutual dependencies and so too are our human and corporate organizations, as well as the communities in which we find ourselves as citizens.

Bill does not think there is any one magical balance that places these three in some kind of idyllic equipoise, but rather that there is shifting and balancing that goes on unendingly. Yet he argues that individuals and businesses do well to recognize these three "extrusions" of nature.[37]

The history of ONB is that of an organization that does, indeed, recognize these three elements. Its identity as a bank provides it with the investment of the economic well-being of the community. Its community dimension orients it to focus on the well-being of those who work for the bank as well as the customers, shareholders, and neighbors with whom it shares citizenship. It knows there are laws to be obeyed, policies to be developed and order that is to be kept.

Community banks, at least in my experience, are often constructed to grasp these three dimensions better than most businesses; indeed, better than most people. And because of this history, the culture and identity of ONB has become oriented to continue to think this way and build on the past while also providing it with the confidence and the corporate permission to do even better. Certainly the stakeholders of ONB believe this, as we shall see in the next few chapters.

Chapter Three

Sincerity and Good Trust

In the summer of 2016, I sent a survey to Old National Bank employees. It was not the typical survey that asks you to rate things the company does on a scale of 1-7 or select from a list of multiple answers. This survey was more open-ended. It asked respondents to share a story that represented the bank to them. This is harder than checking a box on a survey form and I was pleased with the responses I received. At the heart of nearly everyone's response was a sense of how dedicated the bank and its leaders are in attempting to do something that is good. You might call this sincerity or authenticity, and you could certainly place it under the umbrella of integrity that I discussed in the previous chapter. The following survey response exemplifies the answers I received.

> When our bank was bought, the commercial lenders were recruited down to the main office in Evansville for training. While in our training to learn the "ONB Way," our CEO, Bob Jones, made it a point to stop in and visit with us. We were all brand new and had contributed nothing to the bank so far, yet he made us feel by his talk and his mannerisms as if we had already done something good. He was very personable and set the climate as one that is warm, friendly and sincere. He also said "thank you" often and from the bottom of his heart. He also emphasized that we should ALWAYS do the right thing no matter what. I made the comment later that Bob Jones and the rest of his Senior Management Team make us feel like a small community bank even

though we are a $15 billion bank and the largest based in Indiana.

There's much to consider from this statement from an ONB employee. For starters, the fact that CEO Bob Jones' often says "thank you." I've told my kids, when in doubt about what to say, thank you is hard to beat. An attitude of graciousness and gratitude conveys sincerity rather succinctly.

That the CEO of ONB says it "often and from the bottom of his heart" sends a strong message about the culture of the organization as well. That he came across as "warm, friendly, and sincere" and that "he made us feel…that we had already done something good." Those attributes provide a foundation for of integrity, authenticity, and trustworthiness when the CEO "emphasized that we should ALWAYS do the right thing no matter what."

Before I relate other stories that respondents in that survey shared, and before I frame those in a model I use to describe how to build ethical culture, it's important not to come across as arguing that ONB (or any of its individual leaders) are candidates for sainthood. They have flaws; we all do. One of the more sophomoric tendencies of modern debate is that if someone has a flaw, they can't say anything or be an exemplar of good behavior.

You know the drill. If someone dares to advocate for a higher standard or if someone critiques a standard that they believe falls short, a cynic can play the hypocrite card. "Well, who are you to say that when you do X, Y or Z." Since none of us likes to be called a hypocrite, we flinch, and too often, no higher standards are demanded.

As I worked on this book, actress Jennifer Aniston wrote an essay in *The Huffington Post* saying she was "fed up" with the tabloids, in part because of the incessancy of them sticking their cameras in her face every time she walked to a car or airplane.[38] She also objected to the body shaming that tabloids and others in society undertake, especially with respect to women. The tabloids constantly focus on whether or not she is expecting a child, replete with photos of her belly while in a swimsuit with speculation of whether there was a baby bump or not. (I know. You are now asking what in the world Jennifer Aniston has to do with Old National Bank and with business ethics. Stay with me!)

In response, television personality Piers Morgan retorted that Aniston should get off her "high horse" because, at least as I could understand his exceptionally confused and incoherent argument, her beauty has been a major part of her success and editors over time have air-brushed photos of her.[39]

Well, I have never met Ms. Aniston, though we do share a mutual friend. The charge of hypocrisy, however, seems to redirect the conversation from the relevant point. I'm guessing that she is no more of a hypocrite than myself or Mr. Morgan. Even if she is, she makes an important set of arguments about tabloids and the objectification of women. Nevertheless, toss in a charge of being on a "high horse" and we get off track. We're no longer engaged in a subject worthy of our attention; we instead get to fuss over whether Ms. Aniston is or is not a hypocrite. Why should that be the thing we talk about?

We too often make a judgment without facts to support it – what an old ethics professor of mine once defined as "gossiping" – and we use such gossip to distract us (intentionally or unintentionally) from the actual discussion we should have. This is a challenge to any person or company, that advocates for a higher standard of conduct. Raise the charge of a past misconduct and wrap hypocrisy around the person or company, and you don't have to debate the higher standard any more.

There is an old adage: don't make purity the enemy of the good. None of us is pure. We all have shades of hypocrisy and failure. That doesn't mean we can't speak, recognize good conduct or champion the attributes of a good person or company.

I know that ONB makes mistakes, and some stakeholders may have a complaint, but those imperfections should not distract us from recognizing and championing what is, on the whole, a company that does a lot of good things or sincerely attempts to undertake good things.

For many years, I taught a case about an adhesive manufacturing company that did a great number of good things for which it was recognized. In my view, the company really messed up on a big issue and I criticized it for what I viewed as a serious mistake. Yet as I told my students, I looked at the company as an A student who had flunked an exam, so that the company's grade was now a C. It had not suddenly become a hypocritical demon. Indeed, the company continues to do many good things and deservedly has a good reputation now. I still think it really bombed on one issue; that makes the people in the organization human, not hypocrites. It makes the company good, not perfect.

To gain a better sense of ONB's actions, I sent out that survey and asked two simple questions.[1] My first request was for a story about something the employee had witnessed or experienced at ONB that they thought was good, ethical or inspiring. It's an assignment I have used with thousands of students over the years as well as in some consulting work. It's actually a rather difficult task because it's much easier to identify an action that makes you mad or to point out a problem. I generally don't ask respondents to provide the explanation; the stories are still telling because people get to the heart of what moves them.

---

[1] Actually, there were three questions. The last question asked the respondents what color they most associated with ONB. They chose blue. In other places, I have written about a color-coded moral development concept and blue comes out very high on that chart. But it got to be too much to add into this particular book. But you will notice that the cover of this book has a lot of blue in it!

It's much harder to identify a good thing that you find admirable because there is more at stake. We can get mad at just about anything, but when you acknowledge that someone did something you admire, you tap into another level of who you are as a person; you're forced to ponder what you think is good. I make my students then explain why they find actions good and I tell them if they can do this assignment in an hour (it is only a two-page paper), they are either enormously self-reflective or have missed the point.

The second question in the survey asked why the respondent thought Old National was successful, however they defined success. Answering this question provides some insight on the first question, but it elicits deeper philosophical considerations.

When I ask people to describe a good moment, I get a variety of answers of course. Some of the stories take one's breath away, others are rather mundane. There is much to be said about both. There is also much to learn from in these actions.

For example, when I am teaching this assignment to my class, I stop and remark that no one has thrown their coffee or food at me. Nor, do I imagine, that the students have been struggling over whether to throw the coffee or not or, if so, whether to do it at the beginning, middle or end of class. It is something that they've not really considered. There is ethical conduct in their forbearance. It's not dramatic, but it displays a behavior to be admired.

One ONB employee said that he could think of "several things but one that stands out is buying dinner and paying for a person to do a complete house cleaning at my parents' home. They are both homebound and I care for them and don't always have the time to clean."

Simple. Straightforward. Sincere. Old National Bank is not likely to get a huge reward for helping this employee since the favor may not be widely known or likely to be broadcast on a website, press release or newspaper story. Yet it is a good thing for any person, let alone a company, to do. It's something you do when you are sincerely interested in the well-being of an employee.

Similarly, another employee appreciated what Old National Bank had done during the person's service in the National Guard by "making up the difference in my Army National Guard pay when I am gone for my military obligation."

A more dramatic example comes from a grieving employee:

> I have worked in banks for around forty years. In 1996 I lost my partner and had to hide my grief in the work place due to attitudes towards gay people. I started at Old National in 2001. I met someone else in 2005 and life seemed to going well. In 2010, my partner had a stroke and passed five months later. This time my experience was different. Old National supported me in every way. I was allotted the same time off for bereavement as a married couple. My department comforted me with acts of kindness. I was not legally married to my partner at the time. We did have a Holy Union ceremony. I will always remember ONB's kindness and spirit of inclusiveness during a dark place in my life.

Another respondent summarized this sincere commitment

to employees in this way:

> I see ONB doing ethical, inspiring, and good things everyday at my branch. We have such a caring, thorough staff that seeks to help the

customer in times of need. We will go above and beyond...an extra phone call, some extra time researching an item, or staying an extra five minutes to accommodate someone's work schedule...things our staff doesn't have to do, but we do because it is the right thing to do. I left a 20-year career in social services to go into banking, and I couldn't be more pleasantly surprised at the level of integrity and class of the bankers with whom I work!

In 2016, Stanford Business Books released a book I co-authored with Countess Alexandra (Denmark) entitled *The Sincerity Edge*. In our book, we argued that at the heart of ethical conduct is a sentiment of sincerity. There are certainly times in which ethical conduct pays off economically, but there are other times when legal requirements impose socially constructed conditions of behavior so that one has to obey the law.[40] But unless there is motivation to be concerned with personal conduct in the first place, then all the studies and laws don't really make a difference.

We also argued that while it might pay to be ethical, what really makes ethical conduct pay off is when people behave ethically simply because they think it's a good thing and has value in and of itself. At that point, another person can really repose trust in you.

These Old National Bank examples display the moral sentiment of sincerity. There may be payoffs, but they are rather difficult to define, suggesting that ONB behaved the way it did simply because it was a good thing to do. That seems to be the way the people who benefitted understood them as well. Additional stories bear out Old National's commitment to sincerely pursuing good, solid ethical conduct.

For example, one employee noted the prioritization of two key stakeholders: employees (usually referred to as *associates* at ONB) and community investment. By taking care of associates, the employee said, that "takes care of everything else" and by engaging in community investment, the bank creates an "overall strong sense of ethics and doing the right thing [and] creates trust with all groups we touch." In a similar vein, another respondent said that the bank had been successful "mostly for the ethical way/policy that ONB has for all associates in regards to ONB customers/clients and it starts at the top."

Not only does this make sense to me; it is music to my years. Perhaps the most influential approach to business ethics today is the concept of "stakeholder management." A stakeholder is anyone who is affected by a corporate action.[41] That could be just about anyone or anything: employees, customers, suppliers, community, and the environment, not just now but for thousands of years.

There is a solid moral concept supporting stakeholder theory. It's that all human beings (and many would argue non-humans as well) have inherent dignity and should be treated as ends rather than means to an end. Thus, rather than just focusing on shareholders, a company managing under stakeholder theory should manage for everyone.[42]

The challenge of this is how to practically implement something so encompassing. It's hard enough just to look out for the well-being of one set of stakeholders, let alone multiple sets. One approach is to prioritize employees, customers, and shareholders. If you can do that, the other stakeholders will likely be taken care of as well because employees and customers breathe the air, drink the water, and are members of the community. While considering all stakeholders might be difficult, it does seem that it might be manageable, albeit often hard, to manage for this smaller set of stakeholders. In doing so, as the associate said, you'll take care everything else.[43]

Even this commitment, however, can only be maintained with a strong set of moral aims emanating from leadership, which is what the survey respondents recognize. Old National Bank's leadership emphasizes the importance of ethics and exemplifies it in their interactions; and the evidence I've presented so far certainly suggests this. Moreover, it is this commitment to being ethical, as well as the benefits such commitments provide to the associates and community, that make this an interesting company to study. One respondent put it this way:

> I thought it was a good thing that they wanted to be on the World's Most Ethical Company list. It is more important to me than most people because I had a 27-year career with Dun & Bradstreet, who is also consistently on the World's Most Ethical Company list. That I have spent over 30+ years employed by public companies that are consistently recognized on the World's Most Ethical Company list is something that I am proud to acknowledge.

These quotes and the sentiments they expose are what I call Good Trust. Good Trust is part of a larger framework that includes the sincere pursuit of ethical conduct simply because the conduct in itself is independently a desirable thing. It may end up being economically or legally rewarded, but that really isn't the point.

One pursues such conduct because it is good to treat associates well. It is good to be engaged in one's community. It is good to aim to be ethical and to be rigorously evaluated. It is good to have compassion for what employees are going through regardless of whether there is a dollar and cents sign attached to the action. People will trust such an organization, as one of the respondents above said, when folks know that these are your principles.[44]

Good Trust is one of three kinds of trust. It is about striving to be ethical because virtue is its own reward. There are two other kinds of trust as well. Businesses, after all, know there is real value in being trustworthy and there are three ways in which people trust a company.

One reason is that there is a third party that enforces acceptable conduct, as we see with the legal system, the primary example of third party enforcement. It has a coercive requires companies to adhere to certain standards. If they don't, the company can be sued, regulated, or even shut down. I call this **Hard Trust**. This may not be the most inspiring, but it gives us confidence in dealing with businesses.[45]

Real Trust, the third kind, involves treating people well and burnishing one's reputation. Indeed, some companies treat stakeholders well simply in order to have a better public profile. There are clear rewards attached, as there are with community actions as well. Real trust is also exemplified by providing incentives to employees to conduct themselves in the best possible way.[46]

If you put these all together, you end up with a holistic company, one that doesn't just do one good thing but many. This is what Aristotle would term "integrity." It is a kind of business that practices these actions *before* there is an ethical dilemma. By doing so, it *prevents* many dilemmas from arising in the first place. And, when one does – and no matter what any company or person does, there will always be a certain number of ethical dilemmas – the person or company has a better chance of dealing with it well because they have actually *practiced* thinking about these kinds of things.

Looked at this way, ethics is like quality. Quality management teaches us that it is best not to wait until a product or service is completed to do a quality assessment. If you wait until that point, it is too late. If the product or service passes quality inspection, that's great, but if it does not, you face a dilemma: do you take a defective product or service to market (generally not a good idea) or do you go back to the drawing board to get it right (which is expensive). The solution is to discuss and examine for quality throughout product creation or service so that you can solve problems early and create a good product or service. Quality isn't a one-time thing; it's an all-time thing.[47]

Similarly, for ethics, if you never talk about ethics until you are in the midst of a difficult dilemma, your options will be limited: you are likely looking for the least worst solution. After all, that is what makes dilemmas dilemmas: there is no clearly good answer and so you're looking for the least worst solution.

If you never talk about ethical issues until a dilemma is presented, you've probably not developed the skill to resolve such issues. So you are in a doubly bad place. Because ethics hasn't been discussed, a dilemma arises and you don't even know how to have the conversation.[48]

The optimal way to deal with ethics is to make it part of the company at all times by blending Good Trust, Real Trust, and Hard Trust. Talk about the sincere good to be pursued and how this could relate to the business. You can also consider the legal ramifications of the situation. Together, these three kinds of conversations and three kinds of trust become what I call Total Integrity Management. Old National is one of the better companies I have seen in to make this integration and have these kinds of conversations.

It should be no surprise, then, that a company that acts this way produces the following story from a respondent:

> So many stories come to mind, but I will share one that epitomizes the company's compassion and concern for the broader community. Several years ago, a tornado ravaged southwest Indiana in Vanderburgh and Warrick Counties killing 25 and injuring 247 Hoosiers. The devastation was immense. As I spent the first two days on the ground as part of the rescue and recovery, I witnessed hundreds and hundreds of Old National employees working hard in every neighborhood, clearing brush, repairing roofs, cleaning up, working with the Red Cross, and helping families. Obviously, this volunteer work was done on company time and encouraged by Old National Executive Leadership, as long as help was needed.

Here we have a blend of those stakeholders ONB prioritizes: employees and community. What is interesting is that when ONB commits itself to community involvement, it does not just promise and deliver money. As good as that may be – and certainly philanthropy is a good thing – ONB puts skin in the game.[49] That is, it doesn't just give money; its associates roll up their sleeves and sweat in order to help their community. That's a tactile, different approach to community engagement from writing a check, which is why another associate wrote that s/he was "very inspired by ONB's presence in the community. There are hundreds of opportunities for us to be involved to help or inspire others."

The degree to which ONB does this sets it apart from many other companies. Another employee commented on this attribute as well:

This is the only company I have ever worked for that puts so much time and attention into giving back to our community. ONB encourages each of us to go out and make a difference. Each ONB region has a team that brainstorms ideas of how we can give back and what our next project should be. Truly exceptional.

These stories provide ample evidence that the leadership and associates at ONB are committed to ethical conduct simply because they believe that such conduct is a good thing. They demonstrate Good Trust. There is a sincerity with which they approach their work and which will inevitably be felt and appreciated by those with whom they interact, either within the organization itself or during interactions with the community (including customers). Many of the actions reported by the respondents to the survey were not publicized but rather quiet, routine actions that actually demonstrate their authenticity more than a dramatic example might.

Yet there is something to be said for letting others know of your work. After all, there was one stakeholder left out in the comments of the priorities ONB emphasizes. Employee/associates, yes. Community/customers yes.

As a corporation, Old National encourages all associates to volunteer in their communities. Old National then follows through by promoting and advertising all of this volunteer work done by its employees, something I believe a lot of firms fail to do. Many firms encourage volunteering, but that is typically where it ends.

What about the shareholders? Does Old National Bank's way of doing business address their needs too? That's not easy to answer. There are plenty of studies that show that good ethics pays; there is a link between corporate social performance and social financial performance. And while Old National Bank may be a community bank, it is not a non-profit organization or charity.

ONB may pride itself in doing a great number of things for its associates and its community, but it still must stay in business. Moreover, as a publicly held company, its investors are not simply family members who may have other motives in running a business beyond profitability. As a publicly-traded company, Old National Bank is comprised of shareholders who come from many places to obtain a return on their investment.

We'll return to the question of shareholders, but let's revisit the ideas behind hypocrisy. When I interviewed Bob Jones for a previous book I wrote, I asked him if he worried that by talking about ONB's commitment to good actions, the company might become a target for some who just want to point out the failures, even the hypocrisy, that all of us demonstrate sometimes.

His response was refreshing. He acknowledged the risk and that he and ONB weren't perfect. But he also wanted to challenge others to do business this way too because he believed in its importance. So if that means enduring some arrows, so be it. This way of doing business is worth some wounds.

The other reason for talking about these things is that it can help a company's reputation, which can have a positive impact on a third group of key stakeholders: shareholders. We'll start to examine that link in the next chapter on the Good Trust Real Trust Bridge.

Chapter Four

From Good Trust to Real Trust

The difference between Good Trust and Real Trust can be small; any differences reinforce each other. Good Trust is about passion and sincerity. You can trust someone because you know they are deeply committed to doing something good; that's who they are and they see something independently good about being ethical. The last chapter was about how Old National Bank demonstrates its sincerity. Its people seek to do good things because they believe that good things are valuable independent of their legal or economic benefits.

Real Trust is about, well, karma. Being good pays off, especially in the long run. You may act ethically because you sincerely believe it is a good thing to do (Good Trust) but because what goes around comes around and that can be a good thing, there is a payoff to your actions.[50]

Many companies rightly sense this and so see real value in their reputation, in social capital, and in long-term loyal relationships with employees and customers. With Real Trust, ethics pays. That's not bad; in fact it is the mark of a society or a company that has its incentives aligned nicely. We wouldn't want good deeds to be punished, so if ethics pays, that means that some set of values are aligned well. Yes, it is true that benefitting from good conduct means that actions may not be as altruistic as they may appear, but I'll gladly take the tradeoff for a society that rewards good actions.

There is, then, a bridge between Real Trust and Good Trust, which is clear in the survey responses. Consider this statement from one of the employees of ONB:

Recently the Honor Flight of Southern Indiana was taking another planeload of WWII and Korean Veterans to Washington D.C. to see their memorial. At the Northbrook Banking Center in Evansville, the manager and assistant manager volunteered to help with the veterans on the day of the flight. They had to go to training to be able to safely help the veterans in and out of wheelchairs and find out where to direct family members at the airport for the veterans' return. During that training they found out that the organization had to raise $450.00 per veteran to be able to take them on the trip. The two employees decided to try to raise enough money to send a veteran on a flight. With less than two weeks before the flight they decided to take donations and made a patriotic wreath and another item that to raffle off, plus they decided to take donations for the Honor Flight of Southern Indiana. One customer came in and donated enough to pay for a veteran. When they did a final tally from the raffle and other donations they had more than enough to sponsor another veteran. I don't normally drive home by that branch but I did that week and made a deposit, bought some raffle tickets, and donated funds. These things happen every day in different areas of Old National, because we care for people.

There is no doubt in my mind that the effort to support the Honor Flight was genuine and sincere. That makes it Good Trust. But you can also see that these efforts enhanced Old National's reputation, as it should. The two employees were clearly motivated to work hard to make the flight happen and I imagine their passion made them feel good about their work at ONB as well as ONB itself. I'd also be willing to bet that customer loyalty toward the bank deepened. That's Real Trust: A good action has a payoff of improved reputation and loyalty, as it should.

Actions like these strengthen ties between ONB and its stakeholders. From what I can tell, ONB would have supported the Honor Flight anyway, but good actions and deep community involvement also become good business. This chapter shines a light on this bridge: actions that are good in their own right and pursued as independently good things with an awareness that such actions have concrete benefits.

In the book for which I interviewed Bob Jones, *The Sincerity Edge*, my co-author and I interviewed twenty CEOs who already had reputations for commitment to ethical conduct. We were more interested in what these executives thought than what a collection of random executives (some of whom might not care one bit about ethics) thought about important virtues. Here are the results:

Most Important Virtues[51]

	Very Important	Moderately Important	Neutral	Moderately Unimportant
Honesty	100.00% 20	0.00% 0	0.00% 0	0.00% 0
Loyalty	40.00% 8	50.00% 10	10.00% 2	0.00% 0
Sincerity	52.63% 10	47.37% 9	0.00% 0	0.00% 0
Integrity	95.00% 19	5.00% 1	0.00% 0	0.00% 0
Accountability	75.00% 15	15.00% 3	10.00% 2	0.00% 0
Creativity	25.00% 5	30.00% 6	30.00% 6	15.00% 3
Humility	15.00% 3	45.00% 9	20.00% 4	20.00% 4
Efficiency	20.00% 4	40.00% 8	20.00% 4	20.00% 4
Ambition	15.00% 3	55.00% 11	20.00% 4	10.00% 2
Resilience	50.00% 10	25.00% 5	25.00% 5	0.00% 0

Each one of these virtues is a good one regardless of whether someone gets an economic or other type of reward for it.[52] Loyalty received the second most votes. The fact that ambition and efficiency, two virtues that might seem to be crucial to business success, were much lower than the other virtues is an interesting insight into ethical leaders' priorities.[53]

Who would you rather do business with? Someone who has these traits or someone who does not? There is a clear reason to trust people who practice these virtues.

Realistically, people probably practice these virtues with mixed motives. In other words, they believe these virtues are good and also know that others values someone practicing them. This mixed-motive understanding is on display in the following employee's comment about the company's commitment to work-life balance:

> Last year, I received an email from our corporate leadership reminding us how important it is to allow our co-workers to have time with the family and away from the office outside of working hours. This communication also reminded us how hard this is in the era of 24/7 access to email on your phones. We were asked to be respectful and to not send emails outside working hours and when we know team members are on vacation as they will receive those emails and not be able to pull themselves from work. I was struck with how different this message was from other companies I worked for. I have enormous gratitude that I work for a company that puts family time as such a high priority and recognizes that work - personal balance is critical for us to support as a company.

Notice that the worker mentions the good of recognizing the importance of family and work-life balance and is grateful to work for such a company. That's the Good Trust-Real Trust bridge and ONB does it well. The bridge can be seen again with respect to diversity issues in the following quote:

> The one thing that stands out most to me are the efforts and progress we have made as a company in terms of diversity. Having joined the company only a few years ago and having lived in large metro areas for my entire life, I was struck by the lack of diversity, not only at Old National, but within the entire region in which we are based. I remember asking one of the few African American women in Old National what it was like working for the bank as a black woman.
>
> After her initial shock wore off that I even asked such a question, she responded, "Thank you so much for asking." Despite the fact that Old National's employee demographics matched the geographical ones, the executive team felt we needed to do more. We added "Diversity and Inclusion" to our list of company values. We expanded diversity to mean much more than just race. We created resource groups for blacks, Latinos, LGBT, veterans, and the disabled. All these groups are thriving. Each group has an executive sponsor(s) that takes it seriously; all of this is viewed well beyond just "checking the box."
>
> Our board of directors is also much more diverse. Upon my arrival, the board was completely devoid of color. While we had a large percentage of females, any racial diversity of the board was

absent. Since that time, the board added a young, African American male to the board. While this received a positive response, having one person of color on the board can be perceived cynically with an attitude of, "Yup, they made sure they got one." Soon after, another person of color was added. This time it was an African American woman who resides in our banking footprint, but outside of headquarters' location. She is also a veteran.

Today, the company is expanding the scope of diversity and actively seeking ways to better accommodate and find opportunities for the disabled. Many senior executives are being paired up with individuals who are challenged with various disabilities in a mentoring relationship. The change in the makeup of Old National in the few years I've been here has been nothing short of remarkable. At corporate events in town, our teams actually look different from others. When it comes to diversity, this bank on the banks of the Ohio has grown up. And I couldn't be more proud of the progress.

Let me be clear on the two types of good the Good Trust-Real Trust bridge involves. There is a strong value in pursuing an ethical virtue because that virtue is a good thing in its own right. The last chapter emphasized that. There is also an admirable social value when good actions are reinforced by rewards. That is what the next chapter is about.

What this chapter makes note of is that these are two kinds of good that are each valuable in their own right. You do not have to dismiss honesty because it builds a valuable reputation. It is good to try to be honest and it is good that society (through customer and employee loyalty, for example) rewards honesty. Paradoxically, your social rewards may be stronger and more valuable if you practice a virtue for its own good as opposed to wanting social rewards.

Staying solidly on the bridge rather than falling through a not-so-exemplary crack can be difficult. After all, it was the master of political manipulation, Niccolo Machiavelli, who championed the appearance of being good and sincere while scheming all the time. Machiavelli wrote that "[i]t is not, therefore, necessary for a principle to have [virtues such as mercy, faithfulness, integrity, humaneness, sincerity, and religiousness] but it is very necessary to seem to have them."[54]

Well, there's a cynical view. Let me tell you why, as influential as Machiavelli has been for about half a millennium, I don't think he's right.

Norwegian investment banker Per Saxegaard has written of the concept of being *businessworthy* , which means that just as a banker evaluates a loan prospect on the basis of their creditworthiness, so too do we evaluate others on the basis of their moral worthiness. In other words, is this a person you can seal a deal with by a handshake?[55]

Saxegaard argues that the Internet changes our globalized world because it shrinks things and opens communication. We can observe what others are doing. Reputations matter. Five hundred years ago, Machiavelli's Prince was able to control the flow of information. Since that is no longer the case, businesses have reason to be more like my hometown community banks than they might have had fifty years ago, let alone five hundred.[56]

Because it grew from small, community banking roots and expanded in the Internet age, there is an actual, perhaps surprising fit for why the ONB way mirrors Saxegaard's model for financial success in the 21st Century. That's a Real Trust argument and it is also one that one has the greatest karma-like results. In this regard, it is the matching of a sincere good with a karma-like economic results that ONB executes superbly well.

> In 2009, I was a young professional with a small
> family. I had a child at home that was less than
> one year old. In January of that year, an ice storm
> hit the tri-state area that rocked the community.
> A fallen tree ripped the electrical service box off
> my home and I was without power for a full
> week. At that time I didn't have much cash and
> the expense to repair the box was nearly $1000.
> ONB reached out to anyone affected by the storm
> and offered to cover nearly half the expenses to
> ease some of the stress. I couldn't have been
> more grateful. While we are not talking about
> mega bucks, to me at the time it was HUGE!!!!

Small things matter. The habits we put into action every day, the courtesies we don't even think about, such as asking what it's like working at ONB bank as a black woman; these small gestures can be profound.

The survey responses provide ample evidence that such things occur on a regular basis at ONB. $500 in the vignette above is not a lot of money...unless it is at the right time and place for an employee in need. I suspect that that $500 paid off many times over for ONB and I also suspect that the motivation for the gift wasn't calculated to expect a payoff.

One clear identification of the blend of sincerity (Good Trust) and Karma (Real Trust) came from this employee:

> I believe we focus on our associates...what
> they need to be successful and develop
> programs and processes that support them. As
> we have grown and expanded our footprint,
> we have been very focused on
> communication. We do that virtually as well
> as by bringing our teams together physically

so that everyone hears the same message and is able to work and support our strategies because we all know how it supports our continued success.

You may recall that I mentioned that the three key stakeholder groups for a company to value and embrace are the employees, customers and shareholders. Because it is a community bank, ONB sees the good treatment of the community, as well as the employee/associates and customers, as crucial to its strategy of serving its shareholders.

Employees/Associates

Another associate mentioned the time spent with the employees of a bank ONB had acquired:

> In my mind, the event that exemplifies who Old National is came in 2011. Our in-market rival, Integra Bank, was taken over by the FDIC and ONB was chosen as the bank to acquire Integra. Given the tremendous amount of overlap in the companies' respective branch footprints (not to mention back office operations), job losses for the Integra team were going to be tremendous. ONB took steps to partner with Ivy Tech Community College to offer job training, resume writing, and career resource classes to impacted associates so they could find new positions elsewhere. This wasn't something Old National HAD to do, but it was the right thing for these individuals as well as the communities in which they lived - providing resources to employees who, through no fault of their own, found themselves in a situation where their position was no longer needed.

Another bank closing featured prominently with this respondent:

> When Old National Bank closed one of their branches in Southern Indiana, a lady who had been working there for more than 20 years decided to retire instead of moving to another branch. Bob Jones presented her with an additional $3000 for her dedication and service to the bank over the years.

Customers

One respondent summarized ONB's commitment to its customers enthusiastically and succinctly: "We are here for the customers! We help them with their NEEDS! Customers really appreciate our friendliness & will come back because of it." Another associate provided concrete details of exactly what that commitment means.

> I am a Residential Loan Officer with Old National. When someone applies for a home loan, we will lock their rate in for 30, 45 or 60 days. If the loan is not ready to close by the expiration of the lock date and must be extended, if the delay is due to Old National, we will pay for the extension fee to get the rate extended thru the new closing date. Employees are encouraged to pick a not for profit organization that is close to their heart and do volunteer work with that organization. We give back to the Community in that manner. We are moving to a new downtown bank location next week and all the furniture at the old location is being given to Habitat for Humanity to sell in their Re-Store to raise money to build more homes for people who need safe and clean housing and have no way to accomplish that on their own.

Community

ONB's actions toward its employee/associates may often be small and quiet. Good treatment of customers may be more publicly noted, but the examples provided by the survey suggest that these fly below the radar as well. Community engagement, however, is very much out in the open and ONB shines because, as one respondent said, "Old National is there for our community! We have people that volunteer for numerous things in our community all the time!"

While I do not disparage financial philanthropy in any way – to the contrary, I usually celebrate it – there is something special about a company having skin in the game. Writing a check is one thing, but when associates work, sweat, and contribute to the well-being of the community it bonds the associates, the bank and the community in a much deeper way. What is contributed is not cash, but the muscle and spirit of people.

> The simple fact that ONB gives you 2 hours to be part of the community and get involved by volunteering makes it very inspiring. That way we don't only have one story, but thousands of stories of inspiration and motivational events.

ONB brings a smile to its community engagement through activities such as the *100 Men Who Cook* events.

> Every year throughout our footprint Old National hosts various 100 Men Who Cook contests. Bank and community executives as well as local celebrities put on costumes and/or aprons. They cook wonderful food and offer

samples to the attendees. The monies raised go to charity. This is just one example of how Old National gives back to the community.

Other times, the smiles are less community-wide and more family-rich. As one respondent related:

At the branch where I am employed, every department adopts a family for Christmas. The generosity of everyone involved is overwhelming in such a good way. I happened to know an adopted family was amazed what a department of ten accomplished. It was inspirational.

The Good Trust-Real Trust bridge brings a sense of business practicability to ONB's work. It retains its authentic, genuine spirit, but there is an awareness that these good acts may also come around to benefit the company. From these stories, business success has not dampened the pursuit of doing good deeds for their own sake. The awareness of how such deeds can help individuals and the bank further encourages charitable works. That's especially true with ONB's commitment to its associates, its customers, and the community. As we will see, that ends up paying off for its shareholders too.

Chapter Five:

Real Trust

Empirically demonstrating that good ethics is good business is something of a Holy Grail in management education. A colleague once told me that before he died, he was going to empirically prove that good ethics is good business and that bad ethics is bad business. Sadly, he went to his grave without making that case. I suspect quite a few more will follow the same path but not for lack of trying.

No fewer than 80 studies have tried to correlate good ethics with good business or, using different language, corporate social performance and social financial performance.[57] That's enough studies to merit its own study to see how the various efforts have played out. Two business professors did just that: a meta-study of all of these studies.

The results showed that there was a weak correlation between corporate social performance and corporate financial performance, that good ethical conduct slightly tends to lead toward profitability, at least as measured over the long run. Being socially and ethically engaged does not guarantee profits. They are not required in order to be profitable. In fact, one could be a short-sighted jerk and be financially successful.[58]

At the same time, the study shows that you do not have to be unethical in order to be profitable. Some business people believe they need to check their ethics at the door because business is business, it's not a church. Ethics is for family and personal life. The study runs counter to those adages. You can choose to be ethical and enjoy profitability or you can choose to ignore ethical conduct and perhaps still be profitable. There are business strategies associated with both. So what kind of choice should you make?

Old National Bank has clearly chosen to be deeply engaged in the communities where it works and to conduct itself in an exemplary manner as we've seen throughout this book. Has that choice produced success? That is where the category of Real Trust comes in.

Real Trust is about good conduct paying off, which it can do in a few ways. One relates to its external focus. Does truth-telling, promise-keeping, producing high quality goods and services and being engaged in a community improve your reputation and build social capital? Does good treatment of employees, customers, suppliers pay off with increased loyalty and productivity? The second focus is internal. Does an organization reward its employees for doing the good things the organization says it wants them to do or do they reward something different? If it rewards something different, then good actions don't have a payoff.

My mentor LaRue Hosmer gave me a real-life case study early in my career that we called "the bug-infested cookie case." [59] A new employee worked in the gourmet food portion of a department store when they discovered that some of their gourmet cookies were infested with bugs. Her manager told the new employee that they could not throw away the cookies, but instead should sell them at a discount in the inner city. While there may have been character traits that prompted the manager to sell tainted food, which is illegal, not to mention the ethics of such a maneuver, there was logic to her actions.

The manager's commission was based on a formula of profit per square foot of floor space that she controlled. Her future allocation of floor space was based on the same formula. In other words, while I am sure that a gourmet food department would not want its brand tainted by selling bug-infested cookies – that would be a bizarre, brand marketing strategy – the incentives the company provided to its employees encouraged them to do just that. The internal Real Trust question, then, is whether the company is providing rewards for employees doing what they say they want them to do, as opposed to incentivizing them to do something else.

Behind both the internal and external aspects of Real Trust is a belief that good conduct pays off. Does it pay off for ONB? To answer that question, I interviewed Jim Ryan and Lynell Walton, the CFO and Director of Investor Relations, respectively, of ONB. I also compiled some data on my own.

Ryan said that there were some basic measures to assess ONB's financial performance just as there would be for any business. These would include return on equity, return on assets, asset growth, earnings, and stock price among some other, more nuanced statistics. He also indicated that there were other measures of success as well. Yes, those numbers might include satisfied workers and customers and the general esprit de corps of the organization, but he was speaking in more quantifiable terms. Let's take them in order.

Basic Measures of Financial Performance

What I set out below is hardly a sophisticated financial analysis, but it does provide some context for ONB's financial performance. I focus on four categories: Return on Assets, Return on Equity, Asset Growth Rate, and Net Interest Margin, each of which represents key components for banks and provide a good snapshot of a bank's financial performance. All the sources used come from publicly available data, such as the FDIC Quarterly Banking File for the end of 2016. At my request, ONB provided the analysis for the performance of the bank's peer institutions, which are identified in Appendix Four, as well as ONB's performance. I looked at the years 2010-2016 because these mark the years subsequent to the 2009 adoption of ONB's current financial strategy, which further coincides with its recognition as a World's Most Ethical Company.

Return on Assets

The data below shows that ONB's return on assets places it within the average markers of its peer institutions and above average with respect to all FDIC-insured community banks. From 2010-2014, ONB performed well above average in comparison to all FDIC-insured banks. Its performance vis-à-vis its peer institutions ranged from just above to just below average. Looking at overall averages during these seven years, ONB significantly outperformed the FDIC group and was ever so slightly below that of its peer institutions.

FDIC Community Banks[60]		Peer Institutions	ONB
2010	0.21	0.77	0.50
2011	0.55	0.90	0.86
2012	0.83	0.86	1.04
2013	0.90	1.02	1.05
2014	0.93	1.03	0.99
2015	0.99	1.01	0.98
2016	1.01	1.02	0.98
Average	0.77	0.94	0.91

Return on Equity

A similar pattern holds with respect to return on equity, where ONB and its peer institutions outperformed the FDIC group. ONB's performance against its peer group was below average, though nearly all of that can be attributed to the first year – 2010 – with results after that placing ONB just slightly below average. Of course, the aim of a constructing peer group of institutions is, in large part, to challenge the creator of the peer group benchmark do better. In addition, the strategy of growth by acquisition will entail short-term costs that, in a given year, will impact not only ONB's return on equity, but any other bank's so that fluctuation is to be expected. Further, ONB is comparing itself to a successful group of community banks.

FDIC Community Banks[61]		Peer Institutions	ONB
2010	2.07	7.29	4.40
2011	5.19	8.06	7.45
2012	7.68	7.45	8.34
2013	8.27	9.06	8.94
2014	8.45	8.94	7.91
2015	8.85	8.66	7.88
2016	9.06	8.69	7.84
	7.08	8.38	7.54

Asset Growth Rate

The fluctuation issue becomes prominent in the comparison of asset growth rates. Depending on the years in which ONB did or did not make major acquisitions, the asset growth rate necessarily varies. As in the previous charts, if the first year of the comparison, 2010, is excluded, ONB fares well. Indeed, with respect to asset growth, ONB's stands at 13% over the past six years as opposed to its peer institutions' average of 11.15%, which is consistent with the other categories and demonstrates an increasingly positive, competitive position with respect to peer institutions that is well above the FDIC group as a whole.

FDIC Community Banks[62]	Peer Institutions	ONB
2010	-2.24%	6.32%	-9.26%
2011	1.64%	11.67%	18.53%
2012	2.25%	7.81%	10.85%
2013	0.39%	6.42%	0.40%
2014	2.21%	14.12%	21.54%
2015	2.71%	10.11%	2.97%
2016	3.00%	16.79%	23.92%
	1.19%	10.46%	9.86%

Net Interest Margin

ONB exceeds both FDIC and peer institutions' net interest margin averages. While FDIC and peer institutions are virtually identical, ONB's stands above both averages and does so consistently, again with the exception of that first year of the comparison, 2010.

	FDIC Insured Community Banks[63]	Peer Institutions	ONB
2010	3.71	3.81	3.40
2011	3.74	3.86	3.87
2012	3.67	3.77	4.23
2013	3.59	3.64	4.02
2014	3.61	3.65	4.22
2015	3.57	3.54	3.72
2016	3.57	3.52	3.58
	3.64	3.68	3.86

From this brief analysis, we can conclude that ONB's community and ethics-oriented strategy, in the worst case analysis, does not seem to hurt it. It is able to compete very effectively in its market. Of course, other community banks are likely to also be community-oriented, although the quality of that engagement may differ from bank to bank. Even so, we know the quality of ONB's engagement makes it very competitive in its industry and within its peer group and matches well with the empirical research on good ethics being good business and corporate financial performance being linked to corporate social performance. Companies can choose to be ethical – socially engaged – and perform well financially.

ONB prides itself on taking a conservative approach to risk management, which allows it to continue to keep its doors open during a financial crisis, as we have seen is a feature of ONB's history. The caveat to this approach is that a given year may show lower numbers because financial results can depend on the amount of risk a bank is willing to take in any given year. A riskier strategy may well produce higher rates of return in the short term.

ONB does not take a short-term strategy to its financial performance and, as we have already seen, taking a long-term approach is one that opens the door to a more socially engaged and more ethical approach to business itself. Yet a challenge remains. ONB is a publicly traded company. Investors may come from outside a family and outside the community in which ONB operates. Talking about the long-term impact the bank has on its various stakeholders is fine, but investors invest in order to get a return. How does ONB manage the desires of investors?

Ryan responded with two points, first by saying that he and CEO Bob Jones have hundreds of meetings with investors throughout the year that explain in detail what the bank is doing. That level of communication combats misinformation. Moreover, growth-oriented investors are not likely to invest in ONB or in any other community bank. Value-driven investors, however, have a longer-term orientation, prefer less risk, and are more willing to be patient with a long-term strategy.

ONB's aversion to risk, actually, does create something of a rub with these investors, Ryan said. When the bank acquires another bank, there are short-term costs and can sometimes be a concern for those investors, yet they also produce long-term growth.

Additional Measures of Success

Beyond these standard financial measures, Ryan identified four other important measures of the bank's success since the commencement of its 2009 strategy. The first pertains to the transformation of ONB's footprint. Since 2011, the bank has acquired 188 branches, all within the Midwest – specifically Indiana, Wisconsin, Michigan, and Minnesota – mostly in small metropolitan areas, such as Bloomington, South Bend, Columbus, and Fort Wayne, Indiana; Madison and Milwaukee, Wisconsin, and Ann Arbor and Grand Rapids, Michigan. These markets not only show good potential for growth in future years, but they also address a wider demographic and economic issue.

As reported in the *Wall Street Journal*, rural America is struggling significantly, becoming the new "inner city" in the country.[64] Among other worrying trends, such as lack of employment opportunities, increased rates of crime, poverty, divorce, college attainment, disability claims, the opioid crisis, and deaths from cancer and heart disease, rural America is nearing a dubious milestone where more people are dying than are being born.[65] While ONB continues to maintain offices and outreach in these areas, its strategy also incorporates smaller metropolitan areas where it can continue to grow. Thus, its strategy of acquiring smaller banks in metropolitan areas undergirds a long-term foundation for the banks as well as for the communities it serves.

This relates directly to the second measure of success. A community bank with ONB's resources is able to be a better community bank. Provided that it maintains its community orientation, a more robust ONB is able to bring more resources to bear in partnering with organizations in new communities, thereby creating a triple-win for the bank itself, the communities it serves, and the banks it acquires. As Lynell Walton, ONB's Director of Investor Relations, puts it, ONB can make an impact on a smaller community because of its size.

This last institutional benefit may seem surprising but it is important to note as a third measure of success. Banks that have been acquired by ONB, such as Monroe Bancorp of Bloomington, United Bancorp of Ann Arbor, Founders Financial in Grand Rapids, Anchor Bancorp of Madison, Wisconsin, and Tower Financial in Fort Wayne, could have merged with other banks. The fact that they contracted with ONB suggests there were benefits; they could continue to be community banks and employees of the acquired banks viewed their treatment by ONB positively.

Perhaps the summation of these additional measures of success comes from the 2009 strategy in which ONB aims to be relevant to stakeholders. ONB wants to matter to its communities; i is not simply another set of financial resources, but a partner who wants to be involved in its communities.

Future Challenges

How one defines a community bank is not a settled issue, which is important because different rules apply depending on the definition of a community bank. For example, the Dodd-Frank Act places restrictions on certain activities, such as the amount of debit card income, for banks with assets of over $10 billion. crossing the $10 billion Dodd-Frank asset threshold leads to additional regulatory requirements, which carry a significant cost. Compliance with these additional regulatory requirements, and the associated costs, can result in reduced income.[66] Crossing that threshold, as ONB has done, means that the loss of income needs to be made up in other areas, which can result in unintended consequences. For example, if a stable, relatively conservative and reliable source of income is limited, then the bank may need to generate new revenue from other, riskier sources. Thus, the bigger you become, the bigger the pressure to increase risk.

As ONB continues to grow and as Congress debates what defines a community bank, these kinds of issues may proliferate. Does being a community bank mean the bank is small or engaged in the community? If a bank has $2 billion of assets and to satisfy the Community Reinvestment Act, hires an outside firm to place loans in check-the-box kinds of activities without engaging with people in those communities, does that make it a community bank more than a $20 billion bank that actively partners with its stakeholders to have a maximum impact? These kinds of issues further interweave the relationship between complying with the law and executing sound business strategies, a topic of the next chapter.

Chapter Six

From Real Trust to Hard Trust

It is clear that a wide range of stakeholders see Old National Bank as an organization that is community-driven. Employees, customers, and others in the community attest to that fact. Employees take pride in how the bank treats its stakeholders so there is a reason people trust ONB. From all accounts, it appears that ONB employees believe that sincerely engaging with stakeholders is a good thing in its own right.

That engagement has payoffs. ONB's reputation helps it attract employees and customers, which is a benefit to its business. Indeed, it may well be that ONB's sincere belief that being a good citizen is a good thing increases the payoff it receives. People have more reasons to trust it.

Without discounting any of these affective dimensions of ONB and the pride people take in them, ONB's economic sustainability must also include the effective execution of successful banking practices. Those practices, along with these other strong community-based engagements, require a level of institutionalization so they continue rather than erode over time. As one survey respondent put it:

> In spite of the recent banks that we have bought because our Senior Management Team felt the time and the prices were right, we stay focused on good ol' LENDING as our primary bread and butter. A recent Time article proposed that most of the BIG banks were more focused on "trading" and not "lending to small business." Our bank continues to look at the long term perspective which explains why our stock price is not rewarded for steady, continuous service to our customers and our community. We

take the 3 wood off of the tee bed to keep the ball in play instead of "gripping and ripping" to get the quick, riskier drive. Tortoise and Hare lesson: Slow and steady wins the race.

Reinforcing the commitment to be engaged in the community are policies and structures of good governance. This is the bridge between what I call Real Trust and Hard Trust.[67]

Hard Trust is about complying with outside forces that can punish you if you don't meet their expectations. One of those forces is the law. The law is an outside force that makes a business trustworthy because a third party – the legal system – can punish a misbehaving person. A stakeholder, such as an employee, customer, or community, is likely to repose more trust in a person or organization if there is a viable, outside force that will correct misconduct. Thus, you trust the cereal you eat, in part, because there is a food safety regulator – the Food and Drug Administration – that oversees Kellogg and General Mills. This kind of trust is not especially inspiring, but it serves a necessary societal purpose.

Gandhi is reported to have once said that the law is not necessary for 5% of the population because they are going to behave themselves whether there is a law or not. It is also not necessary, he said, for another 5% of the population because they are going to violate social precepts no matter what. The law is helpful, though, for the 90% of the rest of the population who could do with some oversight and nudges to move in the right behavioral direction.

As history demonstrates, financial institutions tend to be in that 90%. (During the mortgage meltdown, one might think that there were a lot in the 5% who wouldn't pay attention to a law anyway!) Since banks are crucially important to a well-functioning economy, there are plenty of laws mandating what banks need to do and ONB, like every other bank, has to comply.[68] But there is another kind of Hard Trust.

Real Trust, remember, is about how good conduct pays off because of the importance of reputation in the market. With Real Trust, you're rewarded for good actions. Be honest, fair, sincere with your stakeholders and there can be a reputational payoff. We have seen this already. But there is a coercive side to reputation; it's the stuff of boycotts and bad publicity. Bad publicity can be as coercive as a lawsuit. [69]

In between Real Trust and Hard Trust – or the bridge between the two – is another bridge that concerns itself with the internal policies that govern the company. Sometimes these are encouraged by legislation, court opinions, and standards from stock exchanges or ratings organizations. How they are implemented – and whether to make the effort subject to an outside certification or ratings – becomes a choice.[70] ONB has made many of these choices in order to institutionalize its identity as a community bank and an ethical and successful business organization.

The way ONB goes about looking at policies is a little different from the way many other businesses do. When you think about policy or law, you may think that some authority enacts a policy and lets everyone know the rules to be followed. That implies a hierarchical governance structure. To be sure, ONB has leaders who do enact, monitor, and enforce policy. But the way that happens is not exactly hierarchical. At the same time, it's not pure democracy either. ONB doesn't have its employee-associates draft policies and rules to follow as if it were an Athenian agora.

For that matter, the very way in which ONB approaches rules and policies is somewhat unique. It fully respects the policies, laws, and rules it must follow, but the entire approach is more what a philosopher might call dialectical. By that I mean that there is a continual loop of conversation about the rules and how well people throughout the organization are abiding by policies; these laws are the starting point in a conversation about how to improve, as opposed to just setting a minimal standard.

For example, ONB Chief Risk Officer Candice (Candi) Rickard oversees thirteen separate functions within the Risk Management Department. Managing risk requires overseeing potential fraud that could expose the company to liability. The department also oversees investigations to get to the facts surrounding any possible non-compliance with the law and corporate policies. At any firm, unpleasant issues may arise because you're looking at the underbelly of the company. The Chief Risk Officer and her staff are likely to see the bad stuff first.

You might think that when a company has a reputation for positive, ethical culture, the job of the Chief Risk Officer might be a little easier. Candi doesn't find it so. Instead, in some ways, it makes it harder.

Why?

ONB encourages employees to speak up and to be free to share ideas and applaud good conduct, as well as to point out times for improvement or when conduct isn't so good. That means the flow of information into Candi's office is high; it might be more than at other places because people care about the ethicality of the culture. Thus, Candi listens to them. Candi enjoys her work at ONB because the reports aren't intended to get others in trouble, but rather to keep the culture of the company vibrantly ethical.

Indeed, this bar of compliance itself is different. Candi reports that there is a bar for what a person is supposed to do pursuant to the laws and regulations of government that the bank must comply with and also internal policies. Following these rules is what a person is supposed to do.

Then there is the high bar, which asks people to go beyond what is minimally required and aims for a higher standard of conduct. Then there is, she laughs, the "Candi Bar," which is the bar she insists upon that aims even higher. Her summary of the Candi Bar is: do the right thing every single time.

Hurdling these bars of conduct calls for something more than rigid application of a rule. It also requires an engagement of the heart. For example, at the time of my interview with Candi, she reported that an anonymous tip had been made that raised an ethical issue involving an employee-associate.

The entire C-Suite group – from legal, fraud, and human resources – met over a period of three days to determine the right call. As Candi put it, a heart was in the middle of their discussion table. That heart belonged to the executive team as they worked to discern the fairest result for everyone involved.

The heart also belonged to the person accused of wrongdoing, because that employee-associate remained a human being for whom they felt responsibility and empathy. It was also their responsibility to be fair to others connected with the bank; they have rights and interests to protect as well.

The heart of the person accused of wrongdoing wasn't going to be thrown under the bus. That's why it took three days of conversation with the executive team – with their hearts on the table – to make sure they knew the right thing to do.

ONB, like other institutions, has laws to follow in order to comply with the alphabet soup of regulators. They have reports to make to the SEC (Securities Exchange Commission), the FDIC (Federal Deposit Insurance Corporation), the OCC (Office of the Comptroller of the Currency), and others as well. Complying with those laws is a good thing, but telling your customers you complied with the law this year isn't a cutting edge marketing tool; it's expected.

Nor does simple compliance warm the heart's embers. Would you go home at night after a long day's work, look across the dinner table at your significant other and say, "Gee, honey. I am so proud! Today, I complied with the Antitrust laws!" Of course not. It is a good thing to comply with such laws, but it's not emotionally inspiring. ONB, however, has found ways to make compliance emotionally inspiring by using the laws as a starting point for recognition. They seek out compliance challenges to become better and use those above-the-law compliance challenges to make a statement about the company to the market.

Old National seeks out other evaluations in hopes of certification, namely external ranking organizations such as the World of Work Seal of Distinction, Volunteer Match, Corporate Engagement Award from the Points of Light Institute, the American Banker Best Banks to Work For, the ABA Foundation Community Commitment Awards, the ISS Governance Quick Score Award, and Bloomberg's Gender-Equality Index.

Of particular note is the Ethisphere Institute, which ONB invites along with others to evaluate how well ONB is doing in its quest to be an ethical company. That's not unusual in its own right, but the way ONB goes about it is.

First, ONB doesn't seek certification in order to meet an external standard per se. They want to be recognized for what they are already doing. It's not as if ONB suddenly decided to be an ethical company and had no idea how to become one; they are already doing a great number of things that define an ethical company.

Knowing they are already doing things for their inherent good (Good Trust), ONB seeks the Real Trust value from recognition for being an ethical company. To get that certification, their policies must be evaluated, which is a Hard Trust issue of compliance.

Second, since no one person or one institution is perfect, ONB is going to learn a few things along the road to certification. The challenge of an external process such as Ethisphere's makes ONB grow.

Third, standards imposed by the law or even by a certification authority like Ethisphere become the next step in ONB's quest to move beyond compliance and toward ethical excellence.

In each of these steps, external laws, rules, certifications, audits, and evaluations become tools to help recognize what the company is already doing well, provide tools for how to get better, and offer a jumping off place for how to aim for something higher. This approach makes a Code of Conduct feel much different than it might be at other places.

Frankly, even though I am a lawyer, I have always been skeptical of companies' uses of codes of conduct. All too often, they strike me as legalistic documents drafted by a General Counsel's Office with the primary, if not sole aim of providing litigation protection or regulatory relief." See, here is our code of conduct!" These codes are often window dressing as opposed to something that makes a difference in the way people do their work.

For example, Enron had a well-written code of conduct but the board of directors simply waived it when Andrew Fastow, its CFO, wanted to obtain ownership interest of a related entity that otherwise would not have been allowed by the code of conduct. Enron could say they followed their code, except when it was inconvenient. Then the board just issued a waiver to get around the code.[71]

ONB doesn't use its Code as Enron did. Dick Dube, ONB's first Chief Ethics Officer, wasn't sure what he had gotten himself into when he took that job in addition to his role of Chief Audit Executive. When he added ethics officer to his responsibilities, he looked around for some guidance. He didn't find much. So he went to an Ethics Officers Association Conference to find out what people were doing.

He met with a consulting company, which offered to grade ONB's code of conduct. ONB got a D-. The consultant offered to write a new code for ONB for a fee. Instead, Dube made the consultant a bet.

"Give me five or six examples of a good code, and I'll write one that gets a B+ or better," he said. "If I can't do it, I'll hire your company." He re-wrote the Code and got a B from the company; he later revised it, added pictures, Q&A, and a cover letter from CEO Bob Jones. Then he mailed it to every person in the company and raised the grade to an A-.

That was the start of things. Dube feels the Code of Conduct is core, but not because it tells people what to do. It became an educational tool and platform from which to aim higher. That trajectory is what led ONB to send ethics messages to all employees every two to three months, to become certified by Ethisphere, and to compete for the World's Most Ethical Company award. Continuing to improve the Code, especially as the company becomes bigger, is the next challenge identified by now-retired Dube and his successor, Joan Kissel.

This continued quest for excellence drives public relations and the corporate social responsibility dimension of ONB. When Kathy Schoettlin, who heads ONB's Public Relations efforts, was first contacted to work for ONB, she laughed. She had been working at the Red Cross for fourteen years and didn't exactly think the banking business was her cup of tea.

But then Bob Jones said to her, "Don't be a banker…worry about the community we serve." Thought of in that way, ONB is in a great position to be able to help many organizations and contribute to the communities where it has its branches, not just financially, but from real engagement with people in the community.

One of the questions I posed to all of ONB's executives related to its growth. Hearkening to my small town roots as well as to my early academic research, I think it makes great sense for companies to be engaged in their communities. But how do you do that if you are in five large states and moving into areas where you haven't had a decades-long presence?

ONB has been rooted in Evansville for over a century and knows its way around Indiana pretty well. But it is new to Ann Arbor, Michigan, Madison, Wisconsin and Rochester, Minnesota. If you're going to claim that you are community bank, how do you do that as you get bigger, larger, and are new in town rather than a long-residing citizen?

Kathy took this question head-on. "We don't just give money," she said. Some banks, in order to fulfill their legal requirements under the Community Reinvestment Act, will hire a syndicator who determines where banks might invest their dollars so they can show a quantifiable engagement with the community on the reports they submit to the alphabet agencies. That's not the ONB approach.

ONB, Schoettlin says, makes sure it is at community meetings and events so they can learn how best to help. They prefer to collaborate and partner with others in the community, even if that's outside their funding priorities and will help in areas that have nothing to do with the banking business per se. They dialogue with the community in order to become part of the community and know how best to help.

Sometimes, that help entails donating money. In 2015, ONB gave more than $5 million in grants and sponsorships. Small actions can make a difference too, such as when ONB paid for the headstone of someone whose family was unable to do so.

They also encourage their employees to volunteer. Kathy stresses that *allowing* employees to volunteer is a good thing, but *encouraging* them to do so takes it a step further.

Being authentic and sincere is crucial in Kathy's view. Programs may build Real Trust. Programs such as *100 Men Who Cook,* which has raised more than $4 million for community activities, needs some level of guidance and continuity for the program to continue in a recognizable and workable form. There is Hard Trust – rules – in that.

But there is still a heart in all of this, just as there is when discussing how to deal with an employee who has made a mistake. Engaging in community activities also requires a heart – an authenticity – so that the program is not a cynical effort to gain business, but a sincere engagement with others.

Kathy traces this commitment to authenticity to Jones himself and also to how the senior management team is itself like a family. You hear a similar message from others on that team as well. For example, Jeff Knight, General Counsel for ONB, notes that he wouldn't want to work at ONB if the company wasn't trying to do the right thing in its work and treating people with dignity and respect. Kendra Vanzo, ONB's EVP of **Associate Engagement and Integration** and head of Human Resources, emphasizes that what is important about policy is how to talk to people about policy. In other words, it is not just the rules, it is what the rules point to about the company and what they mean.

ONB proves a point that I have found hard to make in my own writing. The model I have set out – Hard Trust, Real Trust, and Good Trust – risks being segmented as three different ways to build trust: Following the law, rewarding good actions, and pursuing ethics simply because they are good in their own right. They are not, however, separate. Sometimes I make this approach into a formula:

$$TIM= (HT + RT)(GT)$$

TIM, of course, for Total Integrity Management, which is the name for my model (and which is set out more fully in the Appendix). Notice that to reach this holistic management approach, you have to obey the law and public opinion (Hard Trust), make sure internal incentives for optimal behavior are rewarded (Real Trust) and find a societal payoff.[72]

All the law abidingness and all the incentives don't get you very far unless there is a heart – a desire – to do good. If there isn't, then you're in an Enron situation where codes of conduct are mere words to be waived when inconvenient. If there is no motivation to be ethical in its own right or if Good Trust equals zero, then everything else equals zero.

This demonstrates the extent of my mathematical knowledge.

As we have seen, Old National provides many examples of Good Trust. Good Trust, however, is also part of its approach to creating incentives that reward employees for good actions and it is also why it not only takes complying with the law seriously, but uses the law as an educational tool and jumping off place to further improve the company's culture and its actions.

So, while these three kinds of trust can be analytically separated, they are also inextricably interlinked in a strong ethical culture such as Old National's. You can view the link as a bridge between Hard Trust and Real Trust, but the only reason this bridge exists is because it is constructed with Good Trust as well.

Chapter Seven

Hard Trust

While the NASDAQ (the exchange where ONB shares are traded) requires only that a majority of the directors of the board are independent (that is, not employed by ONB), Old National ensures its compliance by confirming that *all* of its directors except one – CEO Bob Jones –are independent. Since further regulatory requirements insist that members of the Audit, Compensation, and Nominating committees also need to consist of independent directors, ONB's strategy is an efficient one.

Nevertheless, a company could also take a minimalist approach to legal requirements like "majority" and do the bare minimum to comply. That simply doesn't seem like an ONB approach to anything.

A board comprised almost entirely of independent directors, though, faces a structural challenge. The culture of ONB is one that is a mediating institution.[73] That is, the bank generates its own culture as people find great meaning in their everyday interactions with each other, with customers, and with regular suppliers.

Employee-associates feel like members of a family and behave knowing there are consequences to their actions at work. That's not a bad thing; it also doesn't mean someone is overbearingly overseeing them. It means that bringing joy or showing empathy to a fellow employee is rewarding while painful actions require healing.

How can such a culture thrive when nearly all the directors are outsiders? How can outsiders understand the meaningful engagement of everyday work at ONB? How can someone outside your family really "get" the idiosyncrasies of your family? As I found several times through my research of ONB, they think of this question a little differently.

Andy Goebel jolted my thinking with the first thing he said to me over coffee, which was that the board of directors are responsible for the culture of the organization. Not only did he happily shoulder that responsibility as a long-time member of the board and the head of its Audit Committee, but he cited his duty to be responsible for the culture under the regulation by the Office of the Comptroller of the Currency.

The ethics side of me was thrilled to hear him say this, but the lawyer in me found it curious that the board of directors saw its legal duty as creating an ethical culture. Andy quickly connected the dots.

First, he said, you find out how the culture is doing through the internal audit department. He regularly checks in with the chief audit and ethics officer to see how things are going. More importantly, whistleblowers have a direct line to him, outside of any reporting that might take place within the ONB system. So he has a way to find out if there is anything going awry, unfiltered by anyone who might have an interest in covering things up.

Of most importance to Andy is that employees have confidence that someone will listen to what they report. Now, the synchronization kicks in. Time and again, I heard from ONB employee associates and leaders the crucial desire to make sure people are heard when they have complaints. It's true within the staff-driven organization and completely reinforced – and guaranteed – by an independent director. This isn't a case of an outside, remote, independent director not being able to "get" the culture. This is an assurance by an outsider that a shared value would be in place for everyone in the organization.

Not only does this make the culture stronger, but it is also a good bulwark against scandal. Business scandals are often presaged by indications from inside the company that something is amiss, perhaps most famously during the testimony of Sharon Watkins in the Enron debacle. Watkins, among others, knew there was something wrong in Enron's accounting and said so. But no one within the company heard her; or perhaps more accurately, no one was *willing* to hear her.[74]

Making sure employees know that they will be heard is important and knowing that they can directly contact the chair of the board's ethics, reinforces the culture ONB aspires to nourish.

Andy also emphasized the long term. As we have seen, studies about corporate ethics indicate there is a positive correlation between being engaged in a community, being ethical and receiving a financial benefit. We've seen that throughout this book: it's a *good ethics is good business* argument.

Andy had it put to him a bit differently when he served as CEO of one of the predecessor companies which was merged to form Vectren, a utility holding company also headquartered in Evansville. A leading security analyst following the utility industry told him that to run the company well, he should try to please the security analyst because he was too short-term focused.

The good news is that a long-term focus is exactly the strategic horizon a board needs to have in order for the good ethics of everyday ONB life to be rewarded. Moreover, as Jones has said, banking tends not to be a fast-growth industry (unless it's resorting to high-risk tactics) so there is an alignment that reinforces the ONB culture. (Since ONB is the only financial institution to receive six straight Most Ethical Company Awards, it is fair to say that not all banks have figured this out.) As Kendra Vanzo pointed out, this identity also makes it easier to pose a test for every action: is this what a world's most ethical company would do?

There is a third way in which independent directors reinforce rather than muddy ONB's ethical culture. Borrowing from Vectren, which starts each of its board meetings with a safety message, ONB starts every board meeting with an ethics message, placing what is striven for every day right before the members of the board.

With these principles governing the conduct of board members, it is not surprising that lead director Becky Skillman observes the level of respectful and transparent communication between the CEO, the Board, and the Executive leadership team. Further, when the team onboards a new person into one of these roles, it makes sure that person also values respectful and transparent relationships, further enhancing the culture. Indeed, Skillman says that each board member is both bound and enthused by exceeding expectations and doing so in an ethical way.

Skillman had her first contact with ONB shortly after she became Lieutenant Governor of the State of Indiana. Huge tornados hit the southern Indiana area in 2005; 28 people died. When she visited the communities, she was struck by the fact that everywhere she looked, she saw people with ONB shirts cleaning, comforting and feeding the victims. It went on for weeks. She is sure that others were involved too, but ONB stood out.

After she had stepped down as Lieutenant Governor (and after the storm) Becky was contacted by then-chair of ONB's board of directors Larry Dunigan. When she arrived for her first chats with the Board Chair, CEO, and General Counsel, it was *Relay for Life* day at the bank and everyone was wearing tee shirts and planning for the volunteer event on the lawn. She instinctively knew it was a distinctive place with an incredible atmosphere of family and community.

Remember, the notion of Hard Trust is that people will trust an organization because there is an outside third party (usually in the form of government regulation or lawsuits) that keeps it in line. The internal version of Hard Trust is that there are policies and rules for people in the organization to follow and they will be punished if they do not. The "hardness" of Hard Trust is a coercive consequence.

What happens when there is bad news? General Counsel Jeff Knight puts it pretty simply: Bob Jones wants bad news fast. Again, this is not the case with some companies in which no one wants to give the boss bad news. This willingness to face bad news also means it is more likely to be addressed quickly and completely. It also means that tough regulatory laws, such as the Anti-Money Laundering law or the Community Reinvestment Act requirements, aren't dreaded as potentially problematic, but serve as the beginning of a way to exceed what is required.

***

What challenges lie ahead for Old National? Skillman replied to that question with specificity. First is the question of regulation. As administrations change (both federal and state) there will always be changes in regulation that impact a company. Being able to address those and act on them will be an ongoing challenge. That is particularly true now that Old National has now surpassed the $10 billion market in assets, which triggers more regulation the company must contend with.

The second challenge is one that has been in the back of my mind throughout my research on this book: What is the leadership succession plan? Bob Jones has had a remarkable impact on ONB and the culture, which is what drew me to write about ONB in the first place. How will that be sustained over the longer term is a question that very much depends on identifying the right people and further embedding the culture in ONB's history.

A third challenge is keeping pace with technology,

especially given the challenge of cybersecurity. Who could have imagined how much change we have experienced in technology over the past thirty years? What technological changes will we see in the next thirty?

The fourth challenge is risk management. Indeed, Jones has been quoted saying that banking is essentially about risk management. Andy Geobel offered another major challenge: reputation risk. It is important, he argued, for associates to know they work for a company that is trusted. And if ONB's currency is its reputation, then maintaining that trustworthiness in the future will be crucial.

Finally, there is the ongoing challenge of growth generally, especially with respect to the extent to which ONB grows through acquisition. Integrating other banks into the ONB culture will be an ongoing challenge. Skillman shares that some proposed merger and acquisition candidates were not pursued because ONB did not believe that the cultures would mesh.

There is a final point in this discussion of Hard Trust. This chapter is by far the shortest in the book. That's worth thinking about. For many companies, the first line of defense is whether a company is conducting itself within the boundaries or whether its actions are sufficiently supported by some legal argument so that it can avoid punishment. "As long as it's legal, it's ethical" is the way this line of argument would run.

With ONB, complying with the law is still a lot of work. There are many regulations with which a financial institution must comply. There are always potentially unhappy people who might want to file a lawsuit. There are employees who may run afoul of internal policies and of the law itself. But if the rest of the culture is already questing to be ethical and rewarding employees for doing things ONB wants them to do, and if recognizing legal requirements becomes the jumping off platform for doing something bigger and better, then the actual work of complying with the law falls into place much more easily.

Indeed, we can think of this as a challenge for other analyses of companies: The shortest chapter of any book about a good company should probably be Hard Trust. For ONB, there's reason I am ending this chapter so soon.

Chapter Eight

Tone at the Top

It may seem strange that in a book about Old National Bank, where many employee-associates have been quoted along with several individuals from the leadership team and the board of directors, I have not quoted CEO Bob Jones much at all. Yet you've heard his voice at every turn; it just didn't come directly from his mouth.

Every single person I interviewed said that it all starts with Bob Jones. A very large number of survey respondents also specifically identified him as the one who makes the difference. His impact is so large it seems redundant to quote him when everybody does!

Mind you, they are not quoting him because of his power and authority. They are not quoting him because they fear that a megalomaniacal CEO must make the company all about him and that there might be hell to pay if they don't fawn over him. It's the opposite. He has had such an influence on the company because he *doesn't* make it about him at all.

Visit ONB headquarters in Evansville and it is possible that Bob will come out in a nice suit and tie. More likely, he'll walk over to say hello, hand outstretched and face smiling, wearing an old sweater. His modesty, however, does not mask his passion. That reflects the company as well.

***

As I wrote this book, my 93-year-old father-in-law Ed became ill. Before he had to go to the hospital and then hospice, he had signed a power of attorney, giving his daughter (my wife) authority to transact business for him as well as to make health decisions. As a former estate planning attorney, I wanted to make sure all the loose ends were tied up, which frankly may have been a mistake. It caused more work that we needed to do, but then again, it was the right way to do things.

Ed opened an account at Sun Trust in the Virginia suburbs of Washington, DC. We had just moved to the Maryland side of Washington from Michigan and he had moved from New Mexico. When he moved in with us, he did his Sun Trust banking in Silver Spring, Maryland. Six years later, we moved to Indiana. Satisfied with Sun Trust, Ed didn't want to change banks even though there were no Sun Trust branches in Indiana. This worked fine, but when he gave Nancy that power of attorney, I wanted to be sure that Sun Trust knew there would be a new signature on the account, so I called the Silver Spring branch to ask where I should send a copy of the power of attorney.

The representative I spoke with said that Ed would have to stop in to authorize the power of attorney. I responded that he couldn't travel that far and when they said my wife could fly out instead, I said that she had no interest in doing that either. They insisted, however, that she appear in a Sun Trust branch.

The nearest branch to us was in Nashville, Tennessee, about 250 miles away. Coincidentally, my daughter was considering Vanderbilt for college so when we toured the campus, we stopped into a branch bank to get the documents Nancy needed to sign.

From Sun Trust's perspective, we had to look a bit shady. An elderly man opens an account in Virginia, does his banking in Maryland, now lives in Indiana and these people show up saying they want to be able to write checks on his account. I could understand why the Sun Trust folks looked at us a little suspiciously and made us go through some hoops to get things lined up. What we needed was a notary public in Indiana to witness Nancy's signature in order to make everyone happy.

This was easier said than done because when we returned, Ed had deteriorated significantly and had to go to the hospital immediately. From that moment on, we were on a vigil. Nancy was trying to balance the demands of a fairly new job while also spending every second she could with her father.

I sent a note to Scott Shishman, ONB Region President for our area. Though vacationing in Mexico, he sent emails to multiple people within two hours on a Sunday night. Four ONB associates contacted me by 9:00 a.m. the next morning and later that afternoon, one of ONB's notary publics was at Nancy's office to witness the necessary Sun Trust document signing.

I sent a note to Bob to let him know how well his colleagues had performed. I had barely hit the send button and he had another email back to all of them thanking them for stepping up and expressing his pride in the way they performed. He made sure the light shone on them and he was grateful to them.

Three things are worth noting in this vignette. First, ONB associates knew what to do. They acted compassionately and beyond the call of duty. They knew what to do because it was part of ONB's DNA.

Second, the CEO of the company personally thanked all the associates within minutes of hearing about what had happened. That's a personal reinforcement of the ONB culture from the very top.

Third, as Mark Bradford, the former head of Bloomington's ONB region, who had also instilled the tone that influenced the associates who so quickly responded said, "The neat thing is that those associates would have done this for anyone, not just because you (Tim) were on our regional advisory board." Given what I have learned about ONB, I don't question Mark's assessment in the least. The extraordinary thing about what the ONB associates did was that it was *not* extraordinary. It was ordinary. It is what they do. Earlier I wrote that Aristotle said most of our ethical actions are not things we think about. We just do them as habits because they are part of our character. What the ONB associates did might be extraordinary and, indeed, they were. But they were also just the habits of the way the organization operates. The only way things like that happen is when the CEO sets the tone at the top.

***

Jones became Old National's CEO in 2004 and has held the role of Chairman since 2016. Prior to coming to ONB, he served as Executive Vice President of KeyCorp, headquartered in Cleveland, Ohio. He currently serves on the board of Vectren, and is a former board director of the Federal Reserve Bank of St. Louis.

As I've mentioned, I interviewed him for a previous book and asked how he weighs the challenge of leading with a strategy of sincerity and authenticity on one hand while also opening himself up to the scrutiny that comes with saying such an ethic is his goal. He had clearly thought this question through well before; he immediately responded:

> "That is the challenge and the opportunity. That's the leadership responsibility you take if you are going to set off on an ethical course. I'm not going to brag about our good works, but I'm not going to hide them either and I'd hope that by our doing these things, other companies would see what is possible for them to do. If people want to find a flaw in us, they may find one. We're not perfect. But we accept the challenge of living up to what we say we want to be.[75]"

His thinking is directly in line with other CEOs I have interviewed and for whom I have great respect as ethical leaders. As I mentioned earlier, in *The Sincerity Edge*, my co-author and I also interviewed twenty other CEOs and board members in the United States and Europe. They believed that tone at the top was crucial as well and they shouldered the responsibility to make sure they had struck the right tone. As with Bob, those CEOs' tone emphasized humility and commitment to doing the right thing; the rest, they believed, would follow.

Here are the results of their responses to the survey we conducted that asked what factors were important for a company to create an ethical organizational culture.

Most Important Factors

	Very important	Moderately important	Neutral	Moderately unimportant	Very unimportant
Tone at the Top	95.00%	5.00%	0.00%	0.00%	0.00%
	19	1	0	0	0
Listening to all stakeholders	50.00%	33.33%	11.11%	5.56%	0.00%
	9	6	2	1	0
A long-term focus	65.00%	15.00%	15.00%	5.00%	0.00%
	13	3	3	1	0
Clear, well-understood policies and goals	50.00%	45.00%	0.00%	5.00%	0.00%
	10	9	0	1	0
Active engagement of the Board of Directors	30.00%	40.00%	25.00%	5.00%	0.00%
	6	8	5	1	0
Matching employee rewards and incentives with company statements of values, objectives and aspirations	45.00%	45.00%	0.00%	10.00%	0.00%
	9	9	0	2	0
Making CSR about employee involvement in outreach in addition to, or instead of, financial philanthropy	15.00%	35.00%	35.00%	15.00%	0.00%
	3	7	7	3	0

	85.00%	5.00%	10.00%	0.00%	0.00%
Standing behind values even when they appear to cost the company money (at least in the short-term)	17	1	2	0	0
	35.00%	50.00%	15.00%	0.00%	0.00%
Giving internal employees at all ranks the opportunity to share their own stories of positive, ethical behavior that has occurred at work	7	10	3	0	0
	35.00%	55.00%	10.00%	0.00%	0.00%
Giving internal employees at all ranks the opportunity to share their own stories of negative, unethical behavior that has occurred at work	7	11	2	0	0
	0.00%	35.00%	35.00%	30.00%	0.00%
Keeping the size of work groups/teams relatively small so that individuals experience the consequences of their actions on a daily basis	0	7	7	6	0
	50.00%	35.00%	15.00%	0.00%	0.00%
Leadership's articulation of why daily actions make a difference to the well-being of the larger world, extending beyond the company itself	10	7	3	0	0
	55.00%	30.00%	10.00%	5.00%	0.00%
Continuous seeking of new ways to make the company and its culture better	11	6	2	1	0

It is worth noting how well ONB lives up to these factors. Overwhelmingly, our CEOs named tone at the top the most crucial factor. Close behind were standing behind the values even if it may seem to cost the company money in the short term and taking a long-term focus. Other factors were important as well, including the leadership's articulation of why daily actions make a difference to the company and the larger world, which could fall under the umbrella of tone at the top as would clear, well-understood policies, and matching employee incentives with those objectives. In addition, continuously seeking ways to make the company and its culture better, listening to all stakeholders and giving associates the opportunity to voice their negative and positive stories were all important and not likely to happen unless those at the top not just allow but encourage such behavior.

Indeed, when I asked Jones what he would recommend as a key leadership requirement, he mentioned communication and messaging. Constantly reinforcing the message is crucial for sustaining an ethical culture. Thus, all of these traits noted by the executives, while important, have to be communicated in order for them to have an impact. The fact that the ethical and strategic identity of ONB came through clearly in interviews for this book without talking to the CEO first certainly suggests that the messages about ethical culture have gotten through to ONB employee-associates and its other stakeholders.[76]

I am delighted as a professor of business ethics to find models like this that I can share with students. At the same time, academic training includes incorporating a healthy dose of skepticism. My skepticism has often focused on the dangers of transformational leaders.

Lest there be any doubt, Bob Jones is a transformational leader. He changed things. Old National Bank had always been an important member of the Evansville community, but as several interviewees told me, things changed when Bob took over as

CEO. The commitment to customer service, the insistence on honesty, transparency and integrity; and the engagement in community service all went through the roof. That energized the culture and has continued throughout his tenure.

Jones described what happened. He pointed to a nearly 200 year history of ONB as providing a foundation for what he aimed to do as CEO. As we saw early on in this book, that foundation provided resiliency and dependability even in the midst of financial crisis, as well as a strong community foundation. In looking at four key groups a bank serves – clients, employee-associates, community, and shareholders – Jones said he aimed to take ONB "back to the future" to balance these stakeholders. In other words, he aimed to reach into ONB's past commitments to community banking in order to address all the company's stakeholders. In doing so, he simply reinforced the bank's own foundation and history, leading to its current growth and reputation.[77]

Bob is exactly the kind of transformational leader academics love to discuss, They also love to talk about the "simple" need of having a great leader so the rest of the organization will fall behind him or her doing great things. That's fine and inspiring. But there are two concerns about transformational leadership.

The first is that transformational leadership can become arrogant leadership. Someone who is a transformational leader has to have a healthy dose of confidence. The very profile that might produce a transformational leader might also be one that simply likes transforming things rather than aiming toward good. Such a leader may need to have a crisis; if there isn't one, he'll create one.

I don't see that in Jones. Yes, he wants to challenge other companies to integrate good conduct and good business. When I asked him to comment on what others have said in this book, his response was humble. Yes, ONB acquires companies.

When they do, those banks need to be integrated into the ONB culture. But the acquired banks were already selected as being ones committed to community banking principles, so their integration into ONB's culture is one that aligns values quite well.

The second worry about a transformative leader is continuity. Is a transformative leader really capable of handing the leadership mantle off to someone else? Or is leadership so crucial to their identity that they cannot let go? We don't really know the answer to those questions because Jones remains the CEO, with no signs of slowing down. At the same time, the leadership development that appears to be in place at ONB and Jones' own supportive nature certainly suggest that he will not fall into this trap. As Jones himself notes, the board's focus on leadership training and transition further make it likely that ONB continues to balance culture and growth.[78]

I also asked him how he deals with investors who may be more interested in short-term profits than long-term strategy. My experience has taught me that a privately held company, such as a family business, can more easily pursue socially engaging projects because that work is part of the family's identity. If all the family members/shareholders are comfortable being a good community citizen, however the family defines that, then you don't have to worry about other shareholders. Yet anyone can buy a share of Old National Bank. A publicly held company does not structurally enjoy the freedom to pursue community goals in the way that a private institution can. So, how does the CEO talk with investors? Bob thought for a moment and then said:

> Well, you have to have a thick skin. And you have to constantly communicate what you are doing to the investors and to the board and to the other stakeholders as well. Those communications have to be frank, but if we are honestly and continuously communicating to our

stakeholders -especially our investors, then we believe we will have the investors who believe in our strategy.[79]

And what is that strategy? Boiled down to its essence, it seems to be two-fold, both of which are rooted in a keen sense of the identity of the organization. In an interview with BAN, Jones states that ONB does well in mid-market areas.[80] The temptation for banks, he says, is to go into the large metropolitan areas, such as Chicago or Detroit. Not only are those markets "hyper-competitive," but they really don't fit with ONB's identity as a community bank.

In a mid-sized market, however, such as a Bloomington, Indiana, Ann Arbor, Michigan or Madison, Wisconsin, the strengths of a community bank are more apparent. Growth and shareholder value are based on being able to execute a strategy designed and honed by being a community bank, rather than trying to be something else. Those markets, it is worth noting, also feature major universities, which enable the bank to reach a more diverse economic mix, both in terms of students, staff and faculty but also with respect to the commercial lending opportunities that exist at and around academic institutions.

The second part of that strategy is to be a mediating institution for its employee-associates as well as engaged in the community where it is located. That plays to ONB's strengths and has a market advantage. In addition to looking for markets that are mid-sized, ONB has purposefully looked for markets that have a real vitality and energy, and which are experiencing economic growth. College markets like Ann Arbor, Madison, Bloomington, Lafayette and Lexington fit this to a T. Because of the energy and vitality that large universities bring to a community (and because of the proximity of young, bright students), major companies want to be there and build there.

ONB also seeks to expand in places that feel culturally similar to ONB's legacy markets in southern Indiana and Western Kentucky – in other words, markets where business leaders, community leaders, government leaders and private citizens are community-focused. If it feels like an ONB community to Management from a cultural perspective, they are more likely to do a deal. Seeking out these very specific types of communities has allowed ONB to radically transform its footprint over the past five years making it far better positioned to grow organically via commercial lending than we were prior to 2012.

Surprisingly, mathematical models might support this approach. You may think of quantitative trading as devoid of the softer kinds of methods a community bank thrives upon. Jones suggests otherwise. Acknowledging that more of ONB's investors are passive, the growth of ESG (environmental, social, and governance) metrics makes a company like ONB attractive. Having its ethical and other certifications further enhances the attractiveness of the company to ESG models of quantitative trading.[81]

This is not to deify Jones or Old National Bank. They are not perfect, but the old wisdom holds: don't make the perfect the enemy of the good. And they are good.

ONB's model seems to work well. Is it transferable? And if a CEO were to try to replicate or build upon ONB's example, what might Jones advise? He acknowledges that the bank would like to encourage others to practice their work ethically as well.[82] The presence of those ESG investing metrics further supports such a desire.

There is something profound to be said for an institution like a regional bank. These institutions are not Chase, Citi or even Wells Fargo. They are not global behemoths, but $10-100 billion is a big, powerful institution. Among them – for that matter among ALL banks, regardless of size – the fact that Old National Bank was the first to receive a World's Most Ethical Company Award and has now won that competitive award for six years in a row (as of this writing) suggests that there is a way for business – and a pretty big business at that – to show all of us a way to integrate ethics and business. Old National Bank does that.

APPENDIX ONE

TOTAL INTEGRITY MANAGEMENT

(Adapted from *Business, Integrity, and Peace* Cambridge University Press, 2007 & from Vision of the Firm (2nd Edition, 2017, West Academic)

Often, people think of ethics as something associated with a dilemma. In fact, many times, managers think that they go about their work with no ethical implications one way or another until suddenly...they stumble onto a dilemma. Then they have an ethics question.

As an ethicist, I must confess that I find this annoying. Dilemmas are dilemmas because there are no clear answers to them. If there was a clear answer, we would call them something else. But there isn't a clear answer and so we call them a dilemma. If we think ethics are only about a dilemma, then ethics questions are, by definition, questions with no clear answer. And so, managers who view ethics this way come to me (or another ethicist) with a question where there is no clear answer. We tell them that, and they walk away wondering why they ever asked us in the first place!

To be sure, sometimes there are questions where one goes to ask someone who specializes in the field for their advice. That could happen in marketing or accounting or law just as well as it could happen in ethics. Managers legitimately view such people as those who might have some expertise to help them with a problem. Ethicists should be able to make dilemmas more clear. Yet, if we simply leave ethics as co-terminus with dilemmas, we won't get anywhere.

Aristotle believed that many, maybe most, of our ethical actions are those we are unaware of. They are so much a part of our nature and character and we practice them so habitually, we are not even aware of them as being ethics. Yet, they are and because they are, they are resources for us to draw on when we do come across that dreaded dilemma. Indeed, when companies make ethics part of their culture, they tend to more securely embed ethics as habits of their employees and richer ethical competencies are developed as a result. In those kinds of cultures, businesses become trustworthy not because they concocted a dazzling solution to an intractable dilemma but because they are reliably and habitually organizations that make ethics central to their business affairs.

Thus, the better way to look at ethics is in a preventative fashion. That is, how do we prevent problems from developing into dilemmas? The apt analogy is to quality. After a couple of decades of quality theory – ranging from Quality Circles to Total Quality Management to Open Book Management to Six Sigma – it is now well understood that a company does not ensure the quality of a product by waiting until the end of the manufacturing process to perform a quality check. If a company waits until then and there is a flaw, it is too late. The company is then in a dilemma: Does it ship out a defective product or does it swallow the costs of remanufacturing? Neither is a good answer and that is exactly what happens in a dilemma: One merely tries to figure out the least bad answer.

The same is true of ethics. If the first time a company asks about ethics is when there is a bunch of oil in Prince William Sound, it is too late. There is no good way to get millions of barrels of oil out of the water. Exxon had to look for the least bad way of solving the problem. If Exxon was really concerned about oil spillages it would have done more to *prevent* the problem. Like quality, ethics becomes a preventative solution to potential problems by integrating ethics checks throughout the manufacturing process, not just when there is an intractable dilemma.

Why Don't We Get This?

This seems rather straightforward, so why don't companies get it? The answer, I think, is that there are real, perceived detriments to raising ethical issues. In their wonderful work, *The Moral Muteness of Managers*, Fred Bird and James Waters surveyed managers about ethical practices. Bird and Waters concluded that managers have a great deal of moral knowledge, but they fear that by raising an ethical issue at work, they will be viewed as "soft." We all know that one doesn't succeed in business by being soft. One succeeds by being "tough." And so, managers mute themselves.

I don't quarrel with Bird's and Water's research. They are probably right. I do think that it is strange to think of ethics as soft. Three of my moral heroes were Martin Luther King, Jr., Gandhi, and Jesus, and they all got killed. That doesn't strike me as particularly soft. That strikes me that ethics is the tough stuff and the hard work.

Nevertheless, if one wants to improve ethics in business, one has to take into account the accuracy of Bird's and Water's findings. That means thinking about how one can encourage discussing ethics at work and not intimidating those who think it is important. If ethics is built into the daily work of business, we should expect people to get more skilled at thinking about ethics.

Ethics is not, after all, simply an innate trait nor something that stops developing at age six (although detractors of talking about business ethics like to spin these folk tales). Ethics is a skill. If one practices making ethical decisions, one gets better at it. One refines ethical decision-making just as one becomes a better violinist or a better quarterback through rigorous practice. Companies that do this are companies that can be trusted. Companies that do this develop integrity.

An Ethics Equation

How do companies do this? I would like to suggest that they can do this by applying the following formula:

$$EBB = (L_{C/J} + (R_K + J_R + U)\,(M^3)$$

In offering this formula, I must confess great pride. My colleagues in Finance, Marketing, and Accounting have nothing on me. I too have a formula for my classes! Of course, this formula is offered very much tongue-in-cheek. Years ago, I did have colleagues who asked me if I could reduce ethics to a number. Numbers are, after all, hard. Ethics (confirming Waters and Bird) are soft. I thought about this suggestion and thought that there would be something missing if one was able to say that one was, say 22.5 on the ethics scale. Numbers may be "hard" but there are sometimes foundations underlying the numbers that are more important than the numbers themselves. Numbers without foundations are simply arbitrary. The challenge to come up with a formula, though, was too tempting to pass up and it doesn't do a bad job in capturing the academic approaches to corporate responsibility. I borrow the $R_K + J_R + U$ from Bill Frederick, but otherwise, the formula is my own.

The formula stands for the idea that Ethical Business Behavior is the result of complying with the law, provided that the law is just ($L_{C/J}$), attending to stakeholder interests ($R_K + J_R + U$) including attention to notions of rights, justice and utilitarianism, and having motivation to care about either the law or the stakeholders (M^3). If one is faced with making an ethical decision, including a decision about a dilemma, academics use one or a combination of these three approaches. Let me spend a few paragraphs spelling these out a bit more because then I can apply them not reactively, which is what happens when faced with a dilemma-based decision, but proactively when one is trying to create a culture of trust that prevents problems.

It is first worth noting that legally, the duty of managers is to carry out the lawful directives of shareholders. Many think that means profitability and profitability only, but the courts have long upheld the legitimacy of non-financial directives of shareholders. For instance, as law-and-economics scholars Daniel Fischel and Frank Easterbrook have noted, if someone were able to prove that the New York Times could make more money by having racy, front-page headlines rather than adhering to its sense of journalistic excellence, the company could turn its back on the extra profits.

There is nothing illegal about aspiring to journalistic excellence if that is what the shareholders desire. If the Chicago Cubs want to forfeit profits to create a sense of family entertainment by playing more day baseball games than is the norm (as was the case in *Wrigley v Shlensky*), they can do so. If Timberland wants to give its employees time off to work on volunteer causes they can. If Johnson & Johnson wants to jeopardize its brand name in yanking Tylenol off the shelves because it can't live up to its corporate credo, it can. Profitability is essential to the viability of a business, but the law provides a good deal of room to incorporate long-term strategies that may seem initially unprofitable and it also provides room to pursue non-financial directives for their own sake.

Second, most of the action in the field of business ethics is in terms of respect the rights (R_K) of vulnerable stakeholders or pursuing a sense of justice (J_R) or a utilitarian greatest good for the greatest number of corporate constituents. (The subscripts "K" and "R" stand for [Immanuel] Kant and [John] Rawls respectively). This formula is about how business should do its business, but in the process, it shouldn't pollute the environment or sell a product that harms kids for instance, even if in refusing to cause such harms, profitability suffers.

Third, there are typically three reasons why any business will pursue ethical practices: Legal, economic, and moral. Companies pursue ethics because they are motivated by the fear of lawsuits, they see a payoff in good ethics in terms of building social capital, reputation, and goodwill, or they simply want to do something they believe is a good thing to do. That is true if companies are concerned with the misuse of a product and it is true about instances where companies are considering enacting a sexual harassment policy. And so M^3 is about motivation: Why companies institute ethics programs.

This formula can be used to make moral decisions in the midst of a dilemma. But from a preventative standpoint, the formula can be used proactively to create the corporate cultures that enhance trust, integrity, and confidence. Practicing "ethical business behavior" has a reactive feel to it. One is responding to external norms (legal, social, philosophical) for engaging in practices. But if one applies this formula pro-actively, one can create a management approach that integrates ethics in a proactive, leadership model. Then the formula becomes:

$$\text{Total Integrity Management}[83] = (L_{C/J} + (R_K + J_R + U)\,(M^3)$$

The Problems with Integrity and Trust...And Their Benefits

"Trust" and "integrity" are bandied about in business these days with great frequency. Log on to a company's website and it is highly likely that both words will jump off the web page. There is a perception that trust in business is eroding and so in response, business trumpets how this is a time for integrity. What these terms mean is a different story.

Integrity vaguely gets associated with honesty, but it is a much more complex virtue. Integrity, as its root suggests, is about wholeness. An integer is a whole number. To integrate is to bring together. Integrity is not about honesty only; it is about bringing together many relevant virtues and knowing how and when to apply the most relevant ones to a case at hand.

Each approach to business ethics – the legal, the managerial, and the aesthetic spiritual – have something important to say about ethics. In an isolated case, each independently might provide a satisfactory result. For instance, if a company is faced with an issue of product safety, following the law may be sufficient. On the other hand, it may not be sufficient.

To address the complexity of issues that arise in business and to build a "culture" of trust requires more than one single approach. It requires an integrated approach. That integration is one that takes all three approaches and weaves them together. In some sense, this is bad news, because all that weaving takes time and a good deal of thinking of how it should take place for a particular company. Well, welcome to ethics. It isn't necessarily easy, but by breaking these components into "Hard Trust," "Real Trust," and "Good Trust" one can make a lot of progress.

Hard Trust ($L_{C/J}$)

Hard Trust is about coercively requiring corporations to adhere to standards. It is about law and public opinion. An outside third party provides assurances to the public that business will obey certain standards under the threat of punishment if they do not. Hard Trust is about rules. It is about making clear what is permissible and what is not.

In some cases, custom is enough to create Hard Trust. I grew up in a very rural area of the Midwest. You don't need a lot of written rules there because there is great continuity. Families have lived there for generations and everyone understands the authority of unwritten rules. When I go back to my hometown, for instance, I always remember to wave at any car passing me in the opposite direction on the two-lane highways. The reason is that waving is expected and I don't want to be grabbed by my shirt at the Post Office and asked if I am a stuck-up professor now who thinks he is too important to wave at his old friends. I've been gone long enough now that I don't recognize everyone (although I used to be able to) when I go back, but I wave at everyone anyway. That prompts my five-year-old to ask:

"Daddy, who are you waving to?"

I respond, "I have no idea."

"Then why are you waving at them?"

"Because I don't want to die."

Well, I doubt anyone would kill me, but the point is that when there is great continuity, you don't need a lot of written rules. But when you work in a mobile workforce with people moving to a new job every few years and when in a global economy, people you work with come from all kinds of different cultures, then a company needs rules to fairly alert everyone working for them of the rules they are expected to know and abide by.

This is old stuff for companies by now. In large part because of the 1991 Federal Sentencing Guidelines, companies have adopted all kinds of Codes of Conduct, Mission Statements, and Values Statements by which they operate their company. These compliance programs attempt to get everyone at a company to abide by the rules. The Guidelines have been around now long enough so that studies have been done to determine what makes for "effective" (which is the standard the programs are to meet) compliance programs.

Paper programs, of course, don't work very well. But the main problem undermining programs, according to Linda Weaver, Gary Weaver, and their co-authors, is if there is no top-to-bottom accountability. Everyone knows, of course, that lower level workers are accountable to people at the top. But are top level people accountable, if not to the bottom, at least to a code of behavior that everyone from top to bottom must follow? If not, if exceptions are the norm for top management, companies create great cynicism and undermine trust. Let me provide two concrete examples.

Enron had a very well thought-out conflict of interest policy so that high-level executives could not hold ownership interest in related companies. Yet, according to *The Powers Report,* the report of the independent members of Enron's Board of Directors, the Board formally suspended its Code of Conduct three times in order to allow Andrew Fastow to obtain lucrative ownership interests in special purpose entities designed to remove Enron debt from its books and provide a financial windfall for him at the same time. Three times the Board did this! What kind of message does that send?

Or let me give an even more concrete example. In the 1990s, I began to teach Executive Education courses. One evening, I taught a two-hour session on ethics with the main theme being how to make ethics a part of the regular, everyday life of the workforce. I had one fellow, who got very charged up about the whole idea, and with voice rising, fist pounding, and neck veins bulging, he said:

> "I wanna know how my people can know that I mean business! And if they screw up, I'm gonna bust their ass and get 'em out of here!"

It was, to put it mildly, a strange scene. I responded that the best thing he could do would be to make sure everyone knew that the rules applied to him too. He got up and walked out of the room! That's exactly what the Trevino and Weaver studies are showing. Corporate rule and corporate policies are fine, but they have to be fairly and evenly applied or else they boomerang.

From a dilemma-based perspective, when one is in trouble, one asks what is legally required. From a preventative-based perspective, one alerts everyone what the applicable laws are in advance and also carefully designs and publishes policy statements so that people know the rules of the road.

Putting on my lawyer's hat, these programs are essential not only to comply with laws such as Sarbanes-Oxley or the

Federal Sentencing Guidelines, they are essential to give people fair notice of what is expected of them. They need to be accompanied by training programs and measuring mechanisms.

There are two other aspects of Hard Trust. One is public opinion and the other is technological. Law is a coercive weapon to make sure companies behave. So is public opinion. Think of how easy it is today to capture incriminating behavior. How many people have a camera on their cell phone these days? Cameras and communications (Internet, Blogs, television) can turn public opinion against companies very easily, which is why companies today have increasingly developed public relations programs to deal with corporate responsibility.

Cameras are the tip of the technological iceberg. Technology can also make unethical behavior impossible. Think of how companies can simply prevent employees from accessing pornographic websites at work. Technology and public opinion (like the law) are double-edged swords, but the point is that their toughness can be used to force people to abide by certain standards. Used constructively, these tools can be beneficial.

Real Trust ($R_K + J_R + U$)

Real Trust is what most people think of when they think of trust in business. Real Trust is about the business case for building social capital, reputation, and good will through ethical behavior. Real Trust is about aligning rewards and incentives, about garnering the confidence of stakeholders because you keep your word, tell the truth, and produce high-quality goods and services. It is about putting your money where your mouth is, so that when a crunch time comes, you deliver on ethics rather than weaseling out of commitments. It is about making sure that in conducting business, one doesn't trample on the interests of stakeholders who, at the moment of the action, can't protect themselves that well and who trust a company not to do so.

The most lauded case for this is Johnson & Johnson's

handling of the 1982 Tylenol crisis. Let me relate that story a bit differently and personally. In 1982, I was a third-year law student at Northwestern University living in the Old Town area of Chicago. On the corner of North Avenue and Wells, was (and is) a Walgreen's drugstore. When I was feeling under the weather, my preferred medication was Extra Strength Tylenol capsules. One Fall day, I wasn't feeling so well, but discovered that I was out of Extra Strength Tylenol capsules, so I started to put on my coat to go over to the Walgreen's.

Fortunately, my roommate said that he thought he had some in his medicine cabinet, so he went up to his room to check and found some to give to me. While I didn't go to the Walgreen's, that same afternoon, an unfortunate flight attendant from United Airlines did go there and purchased Extra Strength Tylenol capsules, went home to her apartment in nearby Sandburg Village, took them, and died from the poison lacing the pills. Thus, began Chicago's Tylenol killings where seven people died.

No one showed that J&J had done anything wrong – nor have they ever since the case remains unsolved – but within a week, J&J had yanked every bottle of Extra Strength Tylenol off the shelves nationwide. Apparently, the company managers first thought about trying to deny that the company did anything wrong, but then J&Js CEO, James Burke, said that in doing so, the company could not live up to its corporate credo, the first provision of which stressed the obligation of the company to provide safe products to its customers. The company couldn't be sure that it could meet that obligation at that moment and so pulled the product.

Granted, J&J had some good public relations people, but still, making a decision on the basis of some "credo" seems like a very soft way to run a business. And yet, that is exactly what J&J did to its credit. It put its money where its mouth was, not based on a business case – although their actions ultimately proved to be a brilliant business move – but because of a commitment to a certain way of doing business.

Internally, Real Trust is about aligning incentives and rhetoric. It is one thing for a company to claim it values integrity. It is another thing to structure its affairs to actually reward that integrity. For instance, I frequently teach a case I call "the bug-infested cookie case." Written by LaRue Hosmer, the case tells the story of a recent MBA graduate working in a department store in California. One of her jobs was in the gourmet food section, where the story was selling cookies wrapped in sealed foil. Some of the customers said that when they opened the foil, there were bugs crawling around on the cookies. The manager of the gourmet food section told the recent graduate that they would have to get rid of the cookies. The recent graduate thought that meant they were to throw away the cookies. The manager, though, said no, they weren't going to throw away the cookies. She knew of a store in the inner city where they could take the potentially infested cookies, sell them for cents on the dollar, and get back some of their investment.

Now there are a number of things wrong with this scenario, but from a certain twisted standpoint, it made sense. The standpoint was that the manager's annual bonus was based on a formula of profitability per square foot and her annual allocation of floor space was based on the same formula. All the company's incentives were for her to do exactly what she did: Squeeze every cent of profit she could from the product.

I'm sure the store did not want to be known as the bug-infested-cookie-store, but that's exactly what its incentives were leading to. In this case, as in most cases, ethics isn't about personal integrity (although it would have been good for either the recent graduate or the manager to take a firmer stand against the sale of the cookies) and it wasn't about applying a refined philosophical principle. It was about designing a "bad food" category on its accounting books so that the manager wasn't punished for doing the right thing. It is exactly this example that shows that ethics in business is a management issue, not a personal integrity issue.

In the end, J&J's decision was a brilliant protection of its brand, but at the moment of its decision, it was the ethical value more than the "business case" that was important. That value, in fact, was a better business case decision than a business case analysis. It was a value that arose from an enculturation of the corporate credo. J&J practiced its credo in job interviews, games, and evaluations so that it meant something in the daily lives of the company. That enculturation probably headed off a lot of issues that could have ultimately become an intractable dilemma. When J&J was faced with an issue that was not of its making, its culture also generated the way to respond to the problem.

This is not to deify J&J. There are no perfect individuals and there are no perfect companies. At the same time, there is wisdom in its actions. People may trust a company that understands that it can be punished if customers may boycott the product or the government may intercede. But they really trust the company when they know the company is committed to doing the right thing. That leads directly to the final aspect, Good Trust.

Good Trust (M^3)

Good Trust is about caring about ethics. All the legal rules, empirical connections, and philosophical principles in the world only go so far. If people don't care about ethical behavior in the first place, nothing is likely to happen. This is a badly neglected area of business ethics, but it may be the most important one. We tend to be absorbed in the external legal rules to guarantee trust and we want to find a business case for why trust pays. Those are well and good. But the heart of ethical behavior in business gets to how to nourish a sense of caring about the behavior in the first place. That is why in the formula, Total Integrity Management = $(L_{C/J} + (R_K + J_R + U) (M^3)$, if M^3 is zero, everything else ends up as zero.

M³ is about Music, Mediating Institutions, and More Mediating. In other words, it is about Motivation and how that has an aesthetic, sometimes even spiritual aspect, how our moral sentiments are nourished in mediating institutions, and how the aim of how businesses can contribute to sustainable peace (More Mediation) is an inspiring enough "good" to transform how people approach their work.

To illustrate this, I would like to give a really cheesy example. For eleven years, I was a professor at the University of Michigan, an appointment made more interesting because I am an alumnus of one of Michigan's biggest rivals, Notre Dame. I realize that the biggest football game of the year for Michigan has always been Ohio State and that the biggest game of the year for Notre Dame has always been Southern California. But for me, even before I had dual allegiances, I thought that the best college football game each year was the Notre Dame-Michigan game.

They are the two winningest major college programs in football history. Michigan has the most wins; Notre Dame is second. They have been in a virtual dead heat for years in terms of best all-time winning percentage. And in terms of national championships, members of the college football hall of game, and first team All-Americans, Notre Dame is first and Michigan is second. The schools have had legendary coaches, famous stadiums, and even unique helmets. The games are usually very close.

But even if none of this was true, the game is worth going to each year just to hear the two best school songs played all day long. While I know that readers of this article may disagree (and if so, you can simply substitute your favorite rivalry and school songs here), but an awful lot of people will agree that Notre Dame's and Michigan's are the best. John Phillip Souza, the famous "March King" said that Michigan's "Hail to the Victors" was the greatest college march ever written. There is a story that during the Vietnam War, American POWs were unable to talk to each other, but they all knew the tune to the Notre Dame Victory March and so they hummed it. In short, these are just great songs. So here's the test.

Each band (and I have interviewed members of both bands to verify this paragraph's point) have a tradition of first playing the other's song before playing its own. When they play the other's (great) song, you will hear Hard Trust and Real Trust. You will hear all the laws and rules of music followed. You will hear the right notes, right time signature, right key signature, and right rhythm played. The band will do everything "right." That's Hard Trust. You will also see rewards and behaviors aligned. The fans whose band just played aren't going to boo their own band and the fans whose song was just played aren't going to boo their own song. There will be polite applause throughout the stadium as everyone thinks the band did a "nice" thing. That's Real Trust.

Then listen to the band play its own song. When it plays its own song, it plays it with heart, with pride, with passion, and with identity. It is that rendition that sends chills up one's spine. That's Good Trust.

The same is true of business. There are some companies for whom being ethical means following the law. There's something to be said for that. There are others who align their incentives to live up to their rhetoric. There is even more to be said for that. But there are some companies for whom ethics is so much part of the identity of the company and the reason people come to work that ethics becomes a passion for excellence. In those companies, ethics will be talked about on a regular basis and people get good at making decisions. They build a culture so that most ethical problems are headed off before they become problems and even if they still do, the people in the company, like J&J in the Tylenol case, know what to do.

So how then do we get to this place? Do we all go around whistling our favorite fight song? Well, let me give three ways to pursue this quest for aesthetic, even spiritual excellence.

One way is to tell stories. Philosophical and legal principles have their merit, but the most natural way for people to connect with ethical behavior is through telling stories. I play on this inclination with my students. In their first assignment, they have to tell me a story about something they saw in business that they thought was good. Then they have to define what good is. The assignment is just a two-pager, but it is a difficult one. Many students struggle with a memory of the good, preferring to write about something they thought was bad. That's too easy. What's more interesting, and harder, is to define what you think is good. The story part connects them to what's in their heart. The explanation part challenges them to articulate their good in a way so that others can evaluate it, think about it, internalize it themselves, or something else.

Indeed, I have used this in consulting assignments with excellent success. I used the assignment with a family business, a leader in its industry. The family shareholders, however, had come to really dislike each other on, in their words, the ethical issues surrounding the family and the business. After hearing me give a speech, they hired me to come in to help them. It was clear, quickly, that each side thought that I would side with "their side" and against "the other side." I didn't side with anyone.

Instead, I made them do this exercise and then forced them to listen to each other at a weekend retreat. It was painful. It also transformed them because even when the old-style, small-town Calvinists disagreed one of their New Age cousins, they suddenly heard a person with values talking. (The same thing happened when the New Agers listened to the Calvinists.) That "other" suddenly became a person with dreams, values, and goals that were important.

Sometime later, I checked up on them, and they said they weren't sure why they needed to hire me; they all got along so well! I don't have a sophisticated empirical study to prove this assertion, but I believe that if companies put individuals in work groups of fewer than thirty (more on that in a second) and one every three years let those people tell their stories, it would dramatically change the culture of many companies. It would make ethics and values and dreams and goals of everyone relevant to work.

As I argued in my 2001 Oxford University Press book, *Ethics and Governance: Business as Mediating Institution*, a second way to build Good Trust is to take into account our hardwired, biological propensities for interacting with groups and to thereby maximize the expression of our innate moral sentiments. Within the natural law tradition, there is a long-standing belief that human beings form their moral character in "mediating institutions." These are small organizations where is significant face-to-face interactions and people experience, in one form or another, the consequences of their actions. They are family, neighborhood, religious and voluntary organizations, and potentially business too. No matter how much a sibling may make you mad, you have to figure out a way to get along, to be a good citizen of the family. In these structures, our actions become habits and we develop our moral character.

Anthropologists have also shown that there are certain sizes of groups that we are most naturally "at-home" in. The first three of those numbers are 4-6, 30, and 150. For example, the next time you are at a cocktail party, watch how frequently people will talk to each other in a group size greater than 4-6. It will almost never happen (unless there is someone in that group that everyone else believes is super-important and the rest are trying to suck up to that person). If the number in the group gets larger than this, or even gets close to the top numbers, the group will fission like an amoeba. It is simply too difficult to carry on a conversation with numbers larger than this. Some management theorists have applied the same numbers to the maximum number of people a manager should supervise.

The next number is thirty. If one accepts evolution, anthropologists tell us that humans lived in hunter-gatherer societies for about 98-99% of human history. The argument is that our brains have evolved to live in the sizes of groups that comprised that history rather than in large urban areas.

Even today, as explained by Gregory Johnson, there are "scalar stresses" that limit the number of individuals who can work together on a regular basis: Some studies show that in groups of thirty, for every person added to the group, the number of disputes increase not arithmetically for every person added, but exponentially.

Before I learned of this threshold, I frequently noted that the optimum size for an ethics class was thirty. One can still have an entertaining class with numbers beyond that, but there is a community dynamic that is lost once you get above that number. Students are more reluctant to share experiences and to volunteer in larger numbers.

Perhaps my favorite number, though, is 150. Robin Dunbar, an anthropologist in England, tried to figure out why human beings speak better than other creatures. One possible answer is that we have bigger brains. But whales and elephants have bigger brains than we do and we seem to talk better. However, when one looks at head size in comparison to body mass, we have big heads! Look around you! We don't out-run a lion, we don't out-duke a tiger, we out-think them. That is our evolutionary advantage.

Moreover, humans and our primate cousins have a large neocortex in comparison to our body mass. The neocortex is the thin membrane that covers the brain that, somewhat controversially, is believed to be responsible for cognitive processing. The neocortex ratio of primates far exceeds that of other creatures (except dolphins).

Dunbar also possessed data on the sizes of groups primates live in. A given species will only live in a certain size of group. Above that number, the group fissions until it again reaches that ceiling. Dunbar thought there might be a relationship between group size and neocortex ratio, so he plotted the two against each other and then tried to predict the maximum size of a human grouping. The number he came up with was 150.

This is all fun, esoteric stuff, but Dunbar then showed some of its practical dimensions. 150 is the average number of names in an address book. 150 is the average size of the company unit in the military. When Brigham Young moved the Mormons from Nauvoo, Illinois to Utah, he said that he couldn't coordinate 5,000 people, but the people could be organized into groups of 150 and he could coordinate their leaders. Dunbar gives several more examples indicating that 150 represents a maximum of number of individuals who can be in a group where the individuals have an actual, personal awareness of each other. Or as Dunbar colloquially puts it, there are probably 150 in the world who, if you saw them sitting at a bar, you'd feel comfortable pulling up a chair and having a beer with them.

My colloquial example is a wedding. There were 4-6 people who had to be there – bride, groom, witnesses, and officiant. There were thirty that each person thought would just be essential to be on the invitation list. There were about 150 that each thought would be fun to be there and if you get beyond that, the betrothed look at each other and say, "who the hell are they?"

The significance of this is that there are sizes of groups that match our biological comfort levels. Above those levels, we start to lose a sense that our actions make a difference to others, for good or for bad. Listen to someone who got caught embezzling. They will almost always say that they didn't think anyone would pay attention to them – it was such a big place. In smaller groups, one has to care. One has little choice but to know that actions have consequences.

This doesn't mean that one loves everyone in the group, but simply that they have to be taken into account. It also doesn't mean that small groups are more ethical than big groups. It means that moral sentiments of empathy and compassion as well as integrity virtues such as truth-telling and promise-keeping are nourished because they are essential to the maintenance of the relationships in the group. *If businesses want to develop cultures of trust where people are habitually being honest and habitually keeping promises, they need to put employees into small "mediating structures" within the company that match with their neurobiology.*

The more one is in a relationship, the more integrity-kinds of virtues like truth-telling and honesty make a difference. For example, suppose that you had a car with 100,000 miles on it. After driving it for a couple of hours, the car seemed to jerk, as if there might be something wrong with the transmission. Would you feel really, really bad if, when you went to trade the car in for a new one, you didn't mention this possible problem? Some people would. Others would say,

> Car dealers are big boys and girls. They have mechanics. They can look out for themselves. I won't lie that there isn't a problem, but I am not going to pro-actively offer that there is one.

Now suppose that you were me, back in the 1990s and the car I was ready to trade in had 100,000 miles on it. The person I was going to sell it to wasn't a used car dealer, but my wife's 18-year-old nephew. The demands for pro-active honesty go through the roof, if for no other reason than I happened to like Thanksgiving dinner! I didn't want to be carved up by my in-laws after they carved up the turkey because they thought I had taken advantage of the young man. The more one is in an experience of a mediating institution, at work or in a family, the more one has to be concerned with issues of pro-active virtues.

At the same time, more than sentimental caring is needed. Caring sometimes gets limited to other members of the group and precluded from outsiders. That's why just as Hard Trust and Real Trust need Good Trust, so too Good Trust needs the accountabilities to the outside world that Hard Trust (brings through law and public opinion) and Real Trust (though markets) give.

The final aspect of Good Trust is itself a corrective to the negative small groups can generate. That is "more mediation" or, the concept of how to achieve peace through commerce. For several years, I (sometimes with my co-author, Cindy Schipani) have developed evidence that suggests that commonly accepted ethical business practices can reduce the likelihood of violence.

Looking at traits of relatively nonviolent societies identified by anthropologists, political scientists, and economists, it became clear that economic development, adherence to the rule of law (particularly with respect to avoiding corruption) and building good community relations between the company and its host society and also within its own corporate walls were the kind of traits that were championed by ethicists as well. It is not simply that commerce creates peace – businesses sometimes are in the midst of colonialism, imperialism, and project the worst kinds of insensitivities – but rather than a certain kind of business, an ethical business that promotes peace without the negatives commerce has historically brought.

Those practices, living up to responsibilities to shareholders, promoting contract and property rights, avoiding bribery, and encouraging voice, gender equity, and human rights, are consensus-based ethical business practices. And so, it is not that businesses needed to approach business from an entirely different perspective. It is simply that there may be an unexpected payoff to ethical business behavior: It may reduce violence.

Conclusion

Businesses may enhance trust by obeying the law. They may enhance trust by aligning incentives with rhetoric and fostering economic development. But one trusts individuals and one trusts organizations not simply because they *react* to social and market pressures. People truly trust organizations and individuals when they *lead* with moral clarity. Until then, trust is simply responsive and, frankly, risks continually being behind the curve of what society really craves. It is when individuals and companies lead that trust is deeply engendered.

And so, it is good to be ethical and to build trust because one thinks it is a good thing to do. There are also times and places when good ethics can be good business and trust can be reinforced in those happy instances. But companies setting new standards for leadership truly create trust and if companies and their executives need one more reason for being ethical in business, the research now shows that in doing so, they just might prevent a kid from getting his head blown off. I can't think of many more powerful reasons to be ethical today than that.

APPENDIX TWO

OLD NATIONAL BANK FOUNDING AND CURRENT CEO

President Mitchell

Bob Jones

INDEX

Evansville 8, 15, 23, 28, 29, 31, 32, 34, 38, 53, 84, 89, 94, 101

Evansville-Crawfordville Railroad 28, 32

Fastow, Andrew 82, 116

FDIC 29, 61, 67, 68, 69, 70, 71, 80, 142n61-64

Federal Reserve 12, 14, 29, 97

Federal Sentencing Guidelines 115, 117

Federalist Papers 139n1

First State Bank of Biggsville 9

Flood of 1937 139n14

Fort, Timothy 11

Frederick, William 35, 111

Freeman, Edward 141n42

Gandhi, Mohannes 77, 110

George Washington University 11, 12

Goebel, Andrew 88

Good Trust 16, 17, 19, 38, 46, 48, 50, 51, 52, 54, 57, 58, 60, 64 81, 85, 86, 114, 120, 124, 128

Hard Trust 16, 47, 76, 77, 78, 81, 85, 86, 91, 114, 117, 122, 128

Hosmer, LaRue 66, 119

Illinois River 32

Illinois-Michigan Canal 32

Johnson & Johnson 12, 112, 117

ENDNOTES

[1] *See, e.g.* ALEXANDER HAMILTON, JAMES MADISON & JOHN JAY, THE FEDERALIST PAPERS (Ian Shapiro, ed., 2014).
[2] I heard film critic, Michael Medved, make this point at a conference at the University of Notre Dame in 2006, where we were both speakers at an event called "Peace Through Commerce."
[3] Greg Smith, *Why I am Leaving Goldman Sachs*, NEW YORK TIMES (May 14, 2012).
[4] Chairman Bernanke's College Lecture Series at https://www.federalreserve.gov/newsevents/lectures/about.htm
[5] COUNTESS ALEXANDRA CRISTINA & TIMOTHY L. FORT, THE SINCERITY EDGE: HOW ETHICAL LEADERS BUILD DYNAMIC BUSINESSES (2017).
[6] *See,* Ara Parseghian at https://www.ndnation.com/boards/showpost.php?b=football;pid=41071;d=this
[7] *Dred Scott v Sandford*, 60 U.S. 393 (1857).
[8] *On this Day*, NEW YORK TIMES, at http://www.nytimes.com/learning/general/onthisday/harp/1024.html?mcubz=0
[9] *See,* KARL DURINGER, THE FIRST BATTLE OF THE FIRST WORLD WAR :ALSACE-LORRAINE (trans. Terence Zuber, 2014).
[10] *See,* S.C. BURCHELL, THE SUEZ CANAL (2016).
[11] U.S. Department of the Treasury, *Panic of 1873* at https://www.treasury.gov/about/education/Pages/Financial-Panic-of-1873.aspx
[12] Gary Gorton & Ellis Tallman, *How did Pre-Fed Banking Panics End?* (June 9, 2015) at http://faculty.som.yale.edu/garygorton/documents/GortonTallman Paper_June_9_2015.pdf
[13] Historical Collections, Harvard Business School, *Bubbles, Panics & Crashes*, at https://www.library.hbs.edu/hc/crises/1837.html
[14] Indianapolis Star, *Ohio River Flood of 1937* at http://www.indystar.com/videos/news/history/retroindy/2017/08/31/-ohio-river-flood-1937/96498012/

[15] 44 News, *Remembering the Great January 1918 Blizzard*, at http://44news.wevv.com/remembering-the-great-january-1918-blizzard/

[16] National Oceanic and Atmospheric Administration, A Review of the Historic Cold Winter of 2013-2014 at http://44news.wevv.com/remembering-the-great-january-1918-blizzard/

[17] *See,* TIMOTHY L. FORT, DIPLOMAT IN THE CORNER OFFICE: CORPORATE FOREIGN POLICY (2015).

[18] *See,* OLD NATIONAL BANK 150 ANNIVERSARY: FROM EVANSVILLE'S FIRST TO EVANSVILLE'S LARGEST (1984)(hereinafter ONB HISTORY).

[19] *Id.*

[20] *Id.*

[21] Board of Governors of the Federal Reserve, The Community Reinvestment Act at http://44news.wevv.com/remembering-the-great-january-1918-blizzard/

[22] ONB HISTORY, *supra* note 18.

[23] ONB HISTORY, *supra* note 18.

[24] ONB HISTORY, *supra* note 18. (The Canal did reopen in 1853 and remained open for eight years before permanently closing).

[25] ONB HISTORY, *supra* note 18.

[26] ONB HISTORY, *supra* note 18.

[27] ONB HISTORY, *supra* note 18.

[28] Office of the Comptroller of the Currency, *The Bank Secrecy Act* at https://www.occ.treas.gov/topics/compliance-bsa/bsa/index-bsa.html

[29] Office of the Comptroller of the Currency, Comptroller's Handbook: Corporate Risk and Governance (2016) at https://www.occ.treas.gov/topics/compliance-bsa/bsa/index-bsa.html

[30] John Engen, *Drowning in BSA Demands: How to Cope As Regulators Toughen Their Stance on Bank Secrecy Act Requirements* AMERICAN BANKER July 20, 2016.

[31] *Id.*

[32] ONB HISTORY, *supra* note 18.

[33] ONB HISTORY, *supra* note 18.

[34] *See,* WILLIAM C. FREDERICK, VALUES, NATURE AND CULTURE IN THE AMERICAN CORPORATION (1995).

[35] *Id. See, also,* TIMOTHY L. FORT, BUSINESS, INTEGRITY & PEACE: BEYOND GEOGRAPHICAL AND DISCIPLINARY

BOUNDARIES (2007)(hereinafter, FORT, 2007).

[36] FORT, 2007, *supra* note 35..

[37] FREDERICK, *supra* note 34, *see also,* FORT, 2007.

[38] Jennifer Aniston, *For the Record*, HUFFINGTON POST (July 12, 2016)

[39] Piers, Morgan, *My Dear Jennifer, If You are So Fed Up…* Daily Mail Online (July 13, 2016) at http://www.dailymail.co.uk/news/article-3688255/PIERS-MORGAN-dear-Jennifer-fed-having-body-judged-stop-trying-make-look-Photoshop-perfect-magazine-covers.html.

[40] ALEXANDRA & FORT, *supra* note 5.

[41] S*ee, e.g.* R. EDWARD FREEMAN, STRATEGIC MANAGEMENT: A STAKEHOLDER PERSPECTIVE (1984).

[42] *See,* TIMOTHY L FORT, THE VISION OF THE FIRM (2017)(hereinafter FORT, VISION).

[43] TIMOTHY L. FORT, ETHICS AND GOVERNANCE: BUSINESS AS MEDIATING INSTITUTION (2001).

[44] FORT, 2007, *supra* note 35.

[45] FORT, 2007, *supra* note 35.

[46] FORT, 2007, *supra* note 35.

[47] FORT, *supra* note 43.

[48] FORT, 2007, *supra* note 35..

[49] ALEXANDRA & FORT, *supra* note 5.

[50] FORT, 2007, *supra* note 35.

[51] ALEXANDRA & FORT, *supra* note 5.

[52] ALEXANDRA & FORT, *supra* note 5.

[53] ALEXANDRA & FORT, *supra* note 5.

[54] NICOLO MACHIAVELLI, THE PRINCE 93 (Luigi Ricci, trans.; Revised edition E.R.P. Vincent, 1952).

[55] Per Saxegaard, *Are You Businessworthy*? in FORt, *supra* note 42.

[56] Per Saxegaard, *Are You Businessworthy*? in FORt, *supra* note 42.

[57] *See,* JOSHUA DANIEL MARGOLIS & JAMES P. WALSH, PEOPLE AND PROFITS: THE SEARCH FOR A LINK BETWEEN A COMPANY'S SOCIAL AND FINANCIAL PERFORMANCE (2001).

[58] *Id.*

[59] LaRUE TONE HOSMER, MORAL LEADERSHIP IN BUSINESS (1995).

[60] FDIC QUARTERLY, *Quarterly Banking Profile*: *Fourth Quarter 2016* Volume 11 (2017) at 20.

[61] FDIC QUARTERLY, *Quarterly Banking Profile*: *Fourth Quarter* 2016 Volume 11 (2017) at 20.

[62] FDIC QUARTERLY, *Quarterly Banking Profile: Fourth Quarter* 2016 Volume 11 (2017) at 20.

[63] FDIC QUARTERLY, Quarterly Banking Profile: Fourth Quarter 2016 Volume 11 (2017) at 20.

[64] Janet Adamy & Paul Overberg, *Rural America is the new 'Inner City,"* WALL STREET JOURNAL (May 27-28 (2017).

[65] *Id.*

[66] See Christina Rexrode & And Ryan Tracy, *Bank Size Threshold Comes Under Scrutiny,* WALL STREET JOURNAL (May 31, 2017) at B3.

[67] FORT, 2007, *supra* note 35.

[68] FORT, 2007 *supra* note 35.

[69] FORT, 2007, *supra* note 35.

[70] FORT, 2007, *supra* note 35.

[71] *See,* Appendix 1 for an account of this issue.

[72] FORT, 2007, *supra* note 35.

[73] Fort, *supra* note 43.

[74] *See,* Leslie Curwen, *Interview: Sherron Watkins, Enron Whisteblower: The Corporate Conscience,* THE GUARDIAN (June 21, 2003) at https://www.theguardian.com/business/2003/jun/21/corporatefraud.enron

[75] Interview by Timothy Fort with Bob Jones, CEO of Old National Bank, on December 11, 2015.

[76] Interview by Timothy Fort with Bob Jones on June 29, 2017.

[77] *Id.*

[78] *Id.*

[79] *Id.*

[80] Clark Street Capital, *The BAN Interview with Bob Jones, CEO of ONB* (2017) at http://clarkstcapital.com/the-ban-interview-with-bob-jones-ceo-of-onb/.

[81] *Supra* note 75.

[82] *Id.*

[83] Although I like the acronym Total Integrity Management provides, using it, as my wife says, is disturbingly narcissistic.

www.ingramcontent.com/pod-product-compliance
Lightning Source LLC
Chambersburg PA
CBHW062010200326
41519CB00017B/4748